KW-482-271

Contents

Introduction

Hello! We hope you enjoy using this book and that the ideas in it help add to your toolbox of resources for teaching mathematics. The main idea behind "Using Stories to teach Maths Ages 4 to 7" was to provide a way of looking at maths that the children have to learn in school from a fresh angle. This means that their learning can be enhanced by looking at maths ideas in different ways. Using the stories can be a fun way of helping the children with their learning and their revision. It also helps children to understand maths by encountering it in different contexts, such as the imaginary situations in the stories and in real-life situations. Every different way in which a child (or an adult!) comes across a maths concept enhances a child's ability to learn and understand the concept and to remember it. The age categories we have put each story in are of course only a guide as all children are different and they can be of interest and use to older or younger children in the same or different contexts.

About this book

By making maths fun the barriers to learning that they often create ("I can't do maths", "maths is boring" or similar phrases that they may have picked up from others) can be dissolved and the children gain more confidence and facility to understand and use mathematical concepts and this can lead to a far more positive approach and attitude to the rest of their mathematical learning. Certainly having used these stories and poems in many schools around the UK we are confident that the children will enjoy engaging with them and learning from them.

The stories and poems in the book have been written and road-tested over a number of years in schools across the UK. They were originally written using the Mathematics Programme of Study as a guide to provide ideas for pieces we could write. For this reason we hope that between them the stories and poems can provide a resource for initiating or supporting work for many of the learning objectives of the Mathematics Programme of Study. Therefore in the teacher's notes accompanying each piece we quote areas of the Mathematics Programme of Study that are covered by working with them with the children. For several of the first pieces, which are aimed at Foundation/Early KS1 (age 4-6), we have also noted relevant aspects of Early Learning Goals for the Early Years Foundation Stage. In the teacher's notes we also suggest follow up work, often incorporating worksheets or the illustrations that accompany the pieces, which you can use to create a whole lesson around each piece. Of course, suggested lesson plans are only a guide and so you can pick and choose the suggestions and ideas that will work best in your school, with your class etc.

Reading the stories

When you read the children the story we recommend that you read them the story twice. The first time as a story in its truest sense – a story they can listen to and enjoy as a piece of narrative, without it being broken up and dissected as it's told. Hopefully the enjoyment they get from the story will enhance their enjoyment of the mathematics they are learning. However on the first reading of the story, they may have been so involved in the plot etc that they miss some of the maths ideas that are used in the story. So on the second reading you can get the children to focus on the maths ideas that weaved into the story by stopping at the points where a new concept enters into the narrative and discussing its role in the story, using an enlarged copy. This also means that the children will be able to enjoy seeing – and learning from! – the illustrations as well and many of the children will enjoy reading the story with you.

Using the Lesson plans

Within the planning we have added reference statements headed WALT, WILF and TIB as these or similar systems are often used to ensure lessons are focussed, objective led and in context for the learner. They help summarise purpose of the lesson, what is required of the children in order for them to successfully learn that lesson and why what they are learning is important.

 WALT stands for "We Are Learning Today."

 WILF stands for "What I'm Looking For."

 TIB stand for "This Is Because."

The worksheets sheets are designed to support the learning the children are making in mathematics. We recognise that completing them will often require

Using stories to teach

Maths

Ages 4-7

Steve Way & Simon Hickton

Hopscotch
A division of MA Education Ltd

Hopscotch

A division of MA Education Ltd

Published by
Hopscotch,
a division of MA Education,
St Jude's Church, Dulwich Road,
London, SE24 0PB
www.hopscotchbooks.com
020 7738 5454

©2011 MA Education Ltd.

Written by Steve Way & Simon Hickton

Illustrated by Emma Turner,
Fonthill Creative, 01722 717057

Illustrations on pages 85 & 86 by Brian Way

ISBN 978 1 90751 518 7

literacy skills, which in some cases the children will not have at the required level. In order that the work remains focussed on maths we suggest that you, your classroom assistants etc scribe for such children so that their capability in mathematics is not held back by specific difficulties with literacy.

The lesson plans in this book are differentiated particularly where we have included sections labelled "Further Suggestions" that give ideas that within the time constraints of a lesson maybe more suitable for higher attainers to carry out (or get around to!) though all the ideas could be explored to some degree by most children. Also most of the ways in which we recommend follow up to the stories mean that the children are encouraged to carry out investigative work which will be differentiated by the outcome of the children's degree and skill of work.

We hope you enjoy using this book and would welcome all positive suggestions/criticisms that might enhance future volumes!

Finally we'd like to mention that many of the stories are based around a character called the Wise Wizz of Woo. Although many legends, most of them untrue, are told regarding this remarkable character, there are a few that we have been able to establish for certain.

1. Although indisputably wise, he was not a wizard. He was however a wizz at mathematics.
2. He lived a long long time ago (even before teachers were invented in fact – hurray!) hence his need to actually invent number shapes we use today, as none existed before and to then create living numbers and teach them to count in the correct order before being used by people.
3. He had (or has!?!) a time machine.
4. He loved (loves?) strawberry jam. (Hope this helps.)

Contents

How the numbers got their shapes
A poem about how the Wise Wizz of Woo decided what shape they would be.

Maths theme: Exploring numbers 0 - 10

The Numbers learn their order
A story about the numbers from 1 –10 learning to go in the right order when the Wise Wizz of Woo teaches it to them and being awful at it!

Maths theme: Exploring numbers 1 - 10

One to Twenty poem
A way of practicing and learning all the numbers from 1 to 20.

Maths theme: Exploring numbers 1 - 20

How Sir Cylinder saved Prince Pyramid from the Cruel Cuboid Creature for Princess Prism
A poem using lots of the mathematical vocabulary the children are expected to have come across and know (including the names of shapes!)

Maths theme: Mathematical vocabulary (comparisons)

The numbers have a quarrel
After they've finally learned to go in the correct order with the help of the Wise Wizz of Woo, (see "The Wise Wizz of Woo names the numbers") this is a story about ordering numbers from one to ten in different ways.

Maths theme: Exploring features and patterns of numbers using numbers 1 – 10 including odd and even

Ten's problem
Practising and learning order of numbers 10 – 20. Which number can 10 go to 20's party with when 0 will be going with 20? Can the Wise Wizz of Woo help 10 out?

Maths theme: Exploring features and patterns of numbers using numbers 10 – 20 including place value

Joins and splits
Various bands are splitting up and re-forming (how unlike real life!) and different mountaineering teams join up to help each other get to the top of Mount Everest. How many people are in these new combinations?

Maths theme: "Real Life" addition and subtraction

Bernice the Octopus buys a watch
Being an executive Bernice needs a watch but as Carl the Crab asks, which tentacle is she going to wear it on? It's a right ordinal conundrum!

Maths theme: Use of ordinal numbers, times of day

All shapes and sizes
A story about solid shapes including cubes, pyramids, spheres, cones, cuboids, cylinders and prisms. King Cube doesn't like spheres and throws them out of his kingdom. Will he learn his lesson about not liking another type of shape?

Maths theme: 3-D shapes and their properties

Primitive place value

A story about the "invention" of the ten's column in the first school in the world i.e. explaining what each digit in a two-digit number represents/place value. (Miss /a/ is the first teacher in the world to suffer the stress of teaching… but not the last…)

Maths theme: Place value of numbers, simple fractions

Chariot champions

The "invention" of multiplication by Julius Caesar's senators who are fed up of (and terrible at!) working out how many lots of people are competing in a three-man chariot race!

Maths theme: Multiplication as repeated addition

The king-sized take away pizza for the Queen

A story using a lot of subtraction. As all the ovens in the palace have broken down a butler orders a huge pizza for the Queen and her guests. When he arrives he realises that some of each topping will have to be taken away.

With…

I'm counting on you counting back to subtract!

A poem about subtraction using a counting back method.

Maths theme(s): Subtraction including problem solving using subtraction

My problem with pirates

A story involving problem solving; using sequences of addition and subtraction (and some multiplication) up to three steps in order to find the treasure – loads of exciting books about maths! (Oh and some gold and jewels too.)

Maths theme: Problem solving using addition and subtraction problems of more than one step.

Exciting times at the Painthorpe Times

A story using lots of multiplication. The new editor of the paper wants to boost circulation by including reports of as many groups of local groups as possible.

Maths theme: Problem solving using multiplication

Hugh the ostrich detective and the town clowns

A story incorporating problem solving using multiplication to find out which clown the police should invite to their police ball.

Maths theme: Problem solving using multiplication

Sailors setting standards

This story looks at use of non-standard and standard measures (length). The tall "Squares" and the short "Triangles" discover each other on an island they've just discovered and want to measure each other but when they measure each other using bushes they keep getting different results… for some reason…

With…

Sailors setting standards II

This story looks at use of non-standard and standard measures (weight). The "Squares" and "Triangles" want to weigh the presents they've given each other.

Maths theme(s): Measurement, using non-standard and standard units for length and weight (also volume.)

How the numbers got their shape

Early Years Foundation Stage targets
By the end of the Early Years Foundation Stage, most children will be able to:

- say and use number names in order in familiar contexts
- count reliably up to 10 everyday objects
- recognise numerals 1 to 9

KS 1 Programme of Study
Ma 2. 2a. count reliably up to 20 objects…
Ma 2. 2b. create and describe number patterns…

Lesson plan

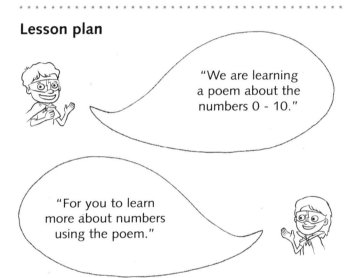

"We are learning a poem about the numbers 0 - 10."

"For you to learn more about numbers using the poem."

To introduce the poem it may be useful to explain some of the facts about the Wise Wizz of Woo explained in the introduction, especially that he lived before numbers existed and in fact it was the Wise Wizz of Woo who realised that we need things called numbers to count with. You can then explain that the Wise Wizz of Woo then had to decide what shape to draw each number and then zero to show that a number was missing and that this poem is about how he decided on each different shape.

You could then read the poem to the children, showing them the illustrations as you do so. Naturally, usually being young and enthusiastic, the children get the idea and chant the name of each number as you reach it. This means that the first thing you could do is teach the children the poem "off by heart." Certainly it has been our experience that the children love doing this.

You could then teach the children to remember which picture goes with each number by presenting them to the children in different orders. They could then play games in groups where the pictures or the numbers are in the wrong order and put them in the correct order against their matching numbers/pictures, which are in the right order.

The children could be given the pictures relating to the numbers in the puzzle form given in the resource section and join up the pieces to make the pictures, which they then place in numbers in order, using the number cards.

Further ideas

The children could be asked to see if they can think of other words apart from those used in the poem, which rhyme with each number. Perhaps they could make up a class/group poem.

The children could make up the shapes of the numbers using sticks etc. Also with reference to the poem they could suggest other ways the different numbers were invented and also be asked to guess how and when the WWW invented 10 based on the clues in the illustration.

Resource section

Number cards with symbol and name on, 1-9 plus zero and 10.

0 **zero**	**1** **one**
2 **two**	**3** **three**
4 **four**	**5** **five**
6 **six**	**7** **seven**
8 **eight**	**9** **nine**
10 **ten**	

In the far far distant past, so long ago even teachers hadn't been invented (hurray!) lived a clever Wizz called "The Wise Wizz of Woo". The Wizz was so clever he invented numbers to do jobs for us like counting and adding up. They are such a useful invention and we are so used to using them we take them for granted. But as they were new when the Wise Wizz of Woo invented them he didn't know what shape to draw them. The way he worked out what shape they should be was written as a story by the ancient poets. Some clever teachers digging deep into ancient piles of paperwork have only recently re-discovered this poem and so you are some of the first to find out for the first time in thousands of years how the numbers became the shapes they are today.

In times long gone by,
(Before you and I.)
The Wise Wizz of Woo,
Invented numbers for you.

But as numbers were new,
He knew not what to do.
He looked round him for clues,
Of shapes he could use.

A dancing hero,
Was how he made ZERO.

A wand that he'd won,
Was how he made ONE.

A river of blue,
Was how he made TWO.

The flight of a flea,
Was how he made THREE.

A pattern of sticks,
Was how he made SIX.

The farmer's barn door,
Was how he made FOUR.

He looked up to Heaven,
And that's how he made SEVEN.

A bird's swooping dive,
Was how he made FIVE.

The eggs on his plate,
Was how he made EIGHT.

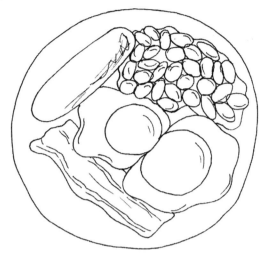

Some ants in a line,
Was how he made NINE.

The number TEN,
He didn't make then,
He'd done his best,
And he needed a rest!

The End

The numbers learn their order

Early Years Foundation Stage targets
By the end of the Early Years Foundation Stage, most children will be able to:

- say and use number names in order in familiar contexts
- count reliably up to 10 everyday objects
- recognise numerals 1 to 9

KS 1 Programme of Study
Ma 2. 2a. count reliably up to 20 objects.
Ma 2. 2b. create and describe number patterns, including odd and even numbers.

Lesson plan

"About counting forwards and backwards to 10 using a story and thinking about odd and even numbers."

"For you to help explore the ideas in the story and think about ways of recognising odd and even numbers."

Just like that wonderful game this could be a lesson of two halves. To begin with you could concentrate on the focus of the story, the numbers getting confused about which order they go in. Secondly you could do investigative work to explore how the Wise Wizz of Woo might have tried to teach the numbers the distinction between odd and even numbers using counters.

Having read the story to the children you could get volunteers to act it out with you. The chosen children could use the number cards from the previous resource to indicate which number character they are playing. Maybe the first time round you could say the number's lines for them but the second time the children could do so.

As the children will probably enjoy the numbers getting their order wrong – though getting it right in the end – you could use this opportunity to point out that it's not

the end of the world if we make mistakes in numeracy, and sometimes it can be quite funny, especially as everyone makes mistakes in maths sometime or other (tell them you sometimes make mistakes too, or at least tell them we do!) All we have to do is laugh about our mistakes and just carry on until we've figured a problem out, if we can. Our numeracy skills should just be a tool to help us deal with problems more easily, not a rod to beat ourselves up with if we don't get things right straightaway. (Sorry, will get off soap box now.)

You could extend the scope of the story by asking the children questions like, "What would the order be if we began at 3?", "What would the order be going backwards starting at 7?" "What would the order be going up in 2's to 20?" etc.

You could then ask the children if they have any ideas about how the Wise Wizz of Woo taught the numbers how to tell the difference between odd numbers and even numbers using counters. Depending on levels of ability you could get some groups of children to see if they can work this out for themselves or you could demonstrate the idea. You could ask particularly precocious groups to see if they can think of different ways of demonstrating/working out the difference between odd and even numbers. They could also work out odds/evens up to 20/30 etc.

Further suggestions

For a more practiced performance of the story, for an assembly for example, the children could paint or draw the numbers to identify themselves/their friends who are taking on the role of a particular number.

You could have a class discussion exploring questions such as, "Why did the Wise Wizz of Woo chose that order?" "What if...he'd chosen a different order?" (These questions would lead nicely into the next Wise Wizz of Woo story "The numbers have a quarrel", where the numbers decide to try out different orders.)

Resources

Number cards from previous story, "How the numbers got their shape".

The Wise Wizz of Woo was trying to teach the numbers the order he had made up for them. The Wise Wizz of Woo had made the numbers come to life after he had decided what shape to draw them but they didn't know what order to go in.

The Wise Wizz of Woo wanted to teach them what order to go in. "You need to know what order to go in so then people will be able to learn to use you in the same order," he had explained to the numbers.

Unfortunately numbers aren't as clever as people, as they are really just tools to help people, so it was taking them quite a long time to learn the order they were supposed to go in. The Wise Wizz of Woo was getting very fed up.

"Right, for the tenth time lets have a go shall we?" said the Wise Wizz of Woo. (For the tenth time.)

"One," said One.

"Two," said Two.

Three and Four looked at each other. They knew that one of them came next but they couldn't remember which one of them it was.

"Er... Four?" asked Four nervously.

"No no no!" said the Wise Wizz of Woo.

"Oh sorry," said Three. "Three."

"Yes... sorry," said Four. "Four."

"Five," said Five.

There was a long pause.

"...Er...is it me next?" asked Six.

"Yes!" said the Wise Wizz of Woo.

"Right then, Six," said Six.

"Seven," said Seven.
"ZZZZZ..." said Eight. She'd fallen asleep again. Eight was always either asleep or thinking about breakfast.

"Eight!!" shouted The Wise Wizz of Woo.

"Um... whashthat??" asked Eight, waking up.

"It's your turn," said Nine. "Hurry up can't you, I'm next."

"Oh great! Is it breakfast time?" replied Eight, not listening properly to Nine. "I'm so hungry! I think today I'll have an enormous bowl of cornflakes, then..."

"No, no no... It's ages since breakfast," said Nine pointedly. "We've all just had lunch – including you. Now will you please say your number, so I can say mine?"

"Oh alright, Eight, then," said Eight and then... she fell to sleep again.

"Nine," said Nine.

"Ten," said Ten.

"Well... well done," said the Wise Wizz of Woo. "That was the best yet... even though it was absolutely terrible. Now that you've finally started to learn how to say your names in the right order from the smallest to the biggest number, there's something else you need to start learning. You need to start learning how to go backwards..."

At this all the numbers began moaning and groaning in despair.

"Do we have to?" asked Four.

"It sounds so much harder than going forwards..." complained Six.

"Yes-we-do," replied the Wise Wizz of Woo through gritted teeth. "Soon you'll have been used so many times forwards and backwards it'll seem completely natural." He continued trying to sound more enthusiastic and up-beat.

None of the numbers thought that could be true but they didn't dare disagree with the Wise Wizz of Woo.

"Off you go then," said the Wise Wizz of Woo."

"Um...Ten," said Ten, pretty sure he was first when they went backwards.

"Nine," said Nine who was the only number who'd understood their order in either way from the beginning.

"ZZZZZ…" said Eight who was still asleep of course.

"Eight!!!" shouted the Wise Wizz of Woo at the top of his voice into Eight's ear.

"AAAAAAGH!!" screamed Eight. "WHAT'S GOING ON??? Oh…" said Eight calming down. "Is it breakfast time? I'm starving. I feel like a really full, full breakfast… I'm going to have a…"

"Noo!" said Nine. "It's still just after lunch time – when you stuffed yourself - We're doing the number order backwards this time, I've just said my number, so as you're before Seven when we go backwards, can you help her by saying your number?"

"Certainly… um, Eight," said Eight. Then she fell asleep once again and had a lovely dream about having seven breakfasts one after the other.

"Seven," said Seven who was glad Nine had said she came after Eight when they went backwards.

"Six," said Six.

"Fi-Fo-ve-ur," said Five and Four together, not knowing who was next.

"It's Five next..." said the Wise Wizz of Woo

as patiently as he could. He wanted to scream.

"Sorry… Five," said Five miserably.

"Sorry… Four," said Four despondently. They both felt really sad because they'd so wanted to get it right.

"Three," said Three.

"Two," said Two.

Everyone looked at One. He was busy looking at everyone else. Finally he realised there was no one else left.

"It's Me!" he shouted excitedly thinking the Wise Wizz of Woo would be really pleased with him.

"What… number… are… you????" screamed the Wise Wizz of Woo hysterically. He was considering giving up and letting numbers be in any old order all the time.

"Oh… er, One...sorry," said One. He was so upset he burst into tears.

"Now, now...there's no need for that," said the Wise Wizz of Woo. He realised that some

practice now is organising you into sets of odd and even numbers," he said. "Do you remember how I showed you how to work out whether you were odd or even using the counters? Let's have the even numbers over here and the odd numbers over there..."

The numbers tried to remember what it was the Wise Wizz of Woo had told them about the counters and how they helped you work out if a number was even or odd - it had seemed completely clear at the time. They tried to arrange themselves into odd and even groups but I'm afraid to say they made a complete mess of it.

The Wise Wizz of Woo nearly screamed at them all again but then he had a better idea.

"What you need is some help," he said. "I'll send you off to whoever's listening to this story and we'll see if they can work it out for you!"

"Brilliant idea!" agreed all the numbers.

of the numbers were doing their best and he needed to give them a rest. Also he realised he couldn't let them go in any old order all the time, as they had such an important job being in the order he'd made up for them. "We'll have a rest from that. What we'll

All the numbers except Eight of course because she was still asleep and dreaming about her next breakfast, even though she'd had twenty breakfasts so far already in her lovely dream.

The End

Early Years Foundation Stage targets

By the end of the Early Years Foundation Stage, most children will be able to:

- say and use number names in order in familiar contexts
- count reliably up to 10 everyday objects
- recognise numerals 1 to 9

KS 1 Programme of Study

Ma 2. 2a. count reliably up to 20 objects… be familiar with the numbers 11 to 20…

Ma 2. 2b. create and describe number patterns… including odd and even numbers…

Lesson plan

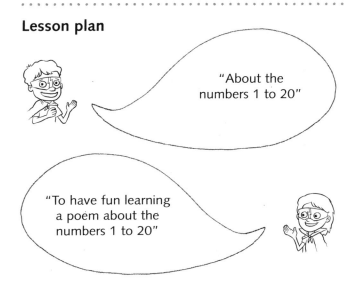

"About the numbers 1 to 20"

"To have fun learning a poem about the numbers 1 to 20"

This is a poem incorporating the numbers 1 to 20, giving the children an opportunity to have fun practising counting up to 20. You could read the poem and present the illustrations to the children first. However the children could be assigned a number, represented by the illustrations provided here and you could run through the poem again, reading the lines for each number with the children and/or getting the children to learn the stanza for "their" number. They could practise the poem for presentation e.g. at an assembly or to another class.

The children could then spend time colouring or painting the illustrations as further preparation for their presentation. You could also see if, as a class or in guided groups, the children could compose their own poems from 1-20… or to a higher number. Poems running in reverse order could be considered as well as poems increasing in jumps of 10's etc.

Further suggestions

You could hand out the illustrations in a wrong order and ask the children to organise themselves in the correct order to present the poem.

You could give a group the illustrations and number cards 1-20 both in the wrong orders and ask the children to organise both into the correct orders, with the number cards matching the correct illustrations.

One to Twenty

One has fun!

Two is blue!

Three's hurt his knee.

Four takes a tour.

Five takes a dive.

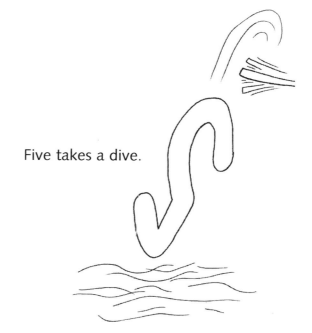

Six buys Pick and Mix.

Seven looks at heaven.

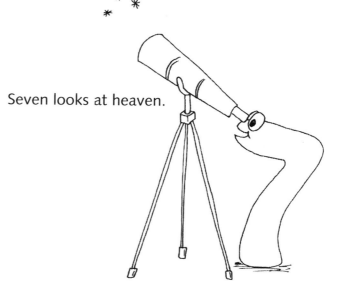

*Using stories to teach **Maths** Ages 4-7*

Eight is always late.

Nine stands in line.

Ten has won again!

Eleven's in heaven!

Twelve like's to dig and delve.

Thirteen is the May Queen.

Fourteen is clean.

Fifteen is not clean!

Eighteen is... Eighteen!

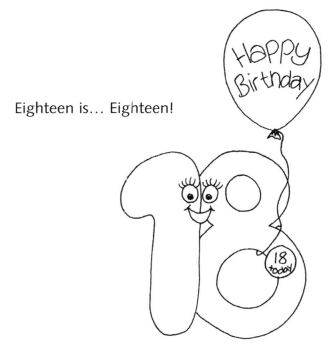

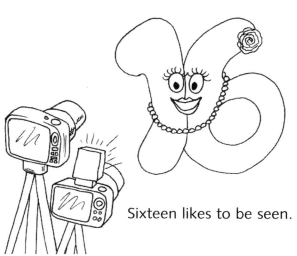

Sixteen likes to be seen.

Nineteen is mean.

Seventeen is keen!

Twenty has plenty!

How Sir Cylinder saved Prince Pyramid from the Cruel Cuboid Creature for Princess Prism

Early Years Foundation Stage targets

By the end of the Early Years Foundation Stage, most children will be able to:

- use language such as "more" or "less", "greater" or "smaller", "heavier" or "lighter" to compare two numbers or quantities

- Use language such as "circle" or "bigger" to describe the shape and size of solids and flat shapes

KS 1 Programme of Study

Ma 2. 1e. use the correct language, symbols and vocabulary associated with number and data.

Ma 2. 1f. communicate in… written form… using informal language… then mathematical language and symbols.

Ma 3. 1d. use the correct language and vocabulary for shape space and measures.

Lesson Plan

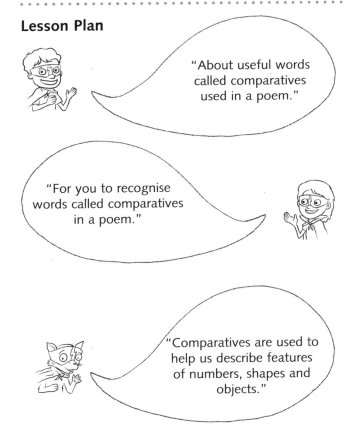

"About useful words called comparatives used in a poem."

"For you to recognise words called comparatives in a poem."

"Comparatives are used to help us describe features of numbers, shapes and objects."

The idea behind this poem was to create a piece using as many comparatives of measure as possible. Whilst reading the poem to the children you could use the illustrations to discuss the meanings of the comparatives, such as longer, shorter and materials you have collected to do so. The children could then be divided into groups/pairs to go on a "Comparative hunt". Each group/pair is asked to look for examples of opposite comparatives, such as bigger/smaller e.g. a big bucket and a small bucket and list them. The most interesting pair could be used towards creating a display made by the whole class of interesting pairs that were found in the "Comparative hunt". Each group/pair must explain their choice. Comparatives you could use are;

- Bigger/smaller
- Larger/smaller
- Thinner/thicker
- Shallow/deep
- Narrow/wide
- Heavy/light
- Long/short
- Straight/curved
- Hard/soft
- Flat/solid
- Stronger/weaker
- First/last
- Full/empty

Though there are loads more and you could get the children to suggest some opposites and then go and find examples!

How Sir Cylinder saved Prince Pyramid from the Cruel Cuboid Creature for Princess Prism

Here my tale does begin,

Full of words, like large, tall and thin.

It tells the tale of the Cruel Cuboid Creature,

(As the villain he does feature),

The creature was both nasty and shallow,

And its viewpoint was deadly and narrow,

You see it liked young princes to eat,

(For it found them nice and juicy and sweet.)

Now Prince Pyramid was a different fellow,

He was handsome, thoughtful, kind and mellow.

But the creature grabbed him out walking one day,

And too his lair stole him away!

Poor Princess Prism she was fraught,

A brave strong Knight was urgently sought,

The princess she did cry and cry,

And rant and rail and call out "Why?"

The moat round the castle got very deep,

For into it did the princess weep.

A Knight at last was to be found,

As the servants looked around.

The Knight he was a man of peace,

(He most enjoyed to play with his niece.)

But the Knight he was quite happy to fight,

If the cause was just and right.

So for a fight the Knight got ready,

(His heavy armour made him unsteady.)

When told of the creature cunning and bold,

The Knight's blood turned first hot, then cold.

He thought his chances they were smaller,

Than of a castle growing taller.

The lake he had to cross was wide,

And he had nowhere to hide...

The Knight drew a sword that was flat and narrow,

And for the beast charged like an arrow!

But the creature slashed his face,

And put the hero off his pace.

Though the creature did not attack him there,

It waited in its woodland lair…

The woodland it was dark and thick...

(Sir Cylinder thought he would be sick…)

He could not tell if he was near...

(But did know he was full of fear!)

As the creature crept up close,

The Knight he turned as stiff as a post!

The creature's claws were cruel and curved,

(For slashing people was how they served.)

The creature's teeth were long and straight,

(And her wicked eyes were full of hate.)

The creature's scales were hard and thick,

As if they had been made of brick!

The Knight fell roughly to his side,

(And wished that he could run and hide.)

But once again he grabbed his sword so solid,

And aimed it at the beast so horrid!

He caught its eye right in its corner,

(Of course she had no one to warn her),

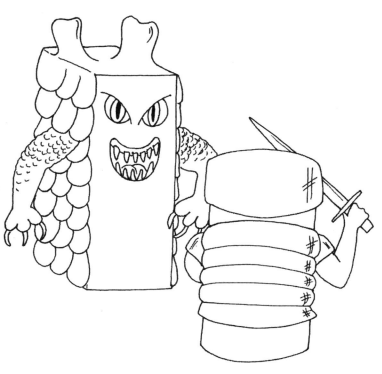

This caused the mighty beast to roar,

Much more than she had done before!

Although she was by far the stronger,

She knew it couldn't fight much longer.

So she raised herself up tall,

(Upon the Knight she aimed to fall.)

But the Knight he struck the creature first,

And so the creature's heart was burst!

The creature it shrank and became smaller,

While the Knight felt he had grown taller!

The creature he had seen his last!

His reign of terror it had past!

The knight shed his armour and felt lighter,

For he had proved he was a fighter.

The prince a captive was no longer,

For the Knight he had proved stronger.

Princess Prism's joy could not be greater!

(She rewarded the Knight a little later!)

His pockets became very full,
(He was heavy and joyful!)

Of fear the land it now was empty,

So it became a land of plenty.

The Knight rode away around the bend,

And so the tale just here must end.

The End

Early Years Foundation Stage targets
By the end of the Early Years Foundation Stage, most children will be able to:

- say and use number names in order in familiar contexts
- count reliably up to 10 everyday objects
- recognise numerals 1 to 9
- talk about, recognise and recreate simple patterns
- use developing mathematical ideas and methods to solve practical problems

KS 1 Programme of Study
2a. count reliably up to 20 objects… be familiar with the numbers 11 to 20…

2b. create and describe number patterns… including odd and even numbers…

Lesson plan

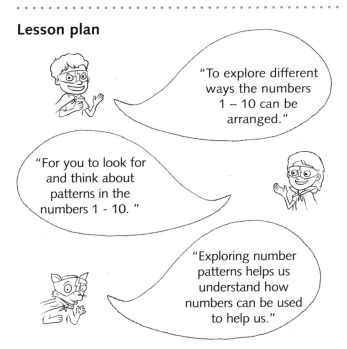

"To explore different ways the numbers 1 – 10 can be arranged."

"For you to look for and think about patterns in the numbers 1 - 10. "

"Exploring number patterns helps us understand how numbers can be used to help us."

If the children are familiar with the Wise Wizz of Woo stories you have read them, you could read the story straight away. If not you might want to just set the story in context by telling the children that the story is set a long long time ago and that the Wise Wizz of Woo had made the numbers come to life, so he could teach them their order of 1 to 10. This proved to be a very difficult job because the numbers kept getting it wrong and number eight was always asleep. The story begins a few days after he had finally taught the numbers their usual order. (The story is divided into two sections; the final section should be read after the

children have experimented with some of the ideas in the story, or ideas they have explored for themselves.)

As you read the first story, as the numbers have different ideas for their new order, you may like to stop and get the children to work out the new number orders as each new idea ("Activity") is introduced, especially if you are working sequentially and want to keep the children focused on one task at a time. However if you are dividing the tasks between different groups you could emphasise how important it is that the Wise Wizz of Woo and the numbers get all the information, so the more straight forward tasks are as important as the more complex ones. The children could work in pairs, groups, or with you as a whole class. The activities we suggest are;

Activity one
The children draw out the numbers (or use the number cards given for the "How the numbers got their shape" lesson) to indicate and work out how many "sticky out" bits they have. The pupils work out the order of the numbers with those with most "sticky out" bits first and those with none last. You may have to mark one of the numbers first, or discuss with the children how they should be marked.

Some of the numbers will have the same number of "sticky out" bits. You could discuss with the children how the numbers in these groups should be arranged. Should it be in the order they would normally come in on the numberline? Or could they investigate the number of ways each group can be arranged and as there are more than one of these groups - all the ways the numbers could be arranged for display/discussion.

Activity two
By drawing the numbers and writing out their names (or using the number cards mentioned above) the children are asked to work out how many letters are in the name of each number and put them in the order with the longest words first and the shortest words last.

The children will discover that several of the numbers have the same number of words in their names. As in activity one you could discuss the way numbers could be arranged in each group and then get the children to investigate all the ways in which they could order the numbers.

Activity three
The children are asked to separate odd numbers and even numbers then put them in order firstly with the even numbers first, secondly with the odd numbers first or vice versa.

As in the activities above, after the children have separated the numbers into odd and even orders, you could ask whether the numbers have to be arranged in order of value in each group and get them to investigate the other possibilities, for example highest value odd numbers first. (The activity builds on the work investigating odd and even numbers associated with our "The numbers learn their order" story.)

Activity four

The children are asked to see if they can think of other reasons for organising the numbers into different orders and finding out what that order would be. The pairs or groups who develop these ideas could demonstrate the order they have thought of to the rest of the class to see whether the other children can work out the idea behind the new order, for example curved shaped numbers followed by straight edged numbers. This activity could be differentiated by you suggesting less complex ideas to a pair/group or you could leave the activity to the pupils to see if they can discover an idea of greater complexity for themselves.

Further ideas

An alternative stimulus could be to ask the children to "Find the order which sounds the worst - which would make the numbers so ill when they say it, it would make them go to bed for a week!" The children could then explain orally the reasoning behind their chosen order!

The children could be asked to make models of the numbers e.g. out of plasticine and investigate how to change one number into another. Or using models and/or paintings of the numbers the children could act out the story - maybe adding their own new orders.

You wouldn't believe the noise in the Land of Numbers! The numbers were having a quarrel! They were quarrelling so loudly they disturbed the Wise Wizz of Woo, who was busy trying to invent minutes and needed to concentrate.

"What's going on?" demanded the Wise Wizz of Woo. "I'd almost decided how many seconds there should be in a minute and now I've forgotten because of all the hullabaloo you're making! Blast… was it 5… 17… or 60?"

"Sorry," said all the numbers except Eight.

"ZZZZ," said Eight. She was asleep as usual.

"What are you quarrelling about anyway?" asked the Wise Wizz of Woo.

All of the numbers looked embarrassed. Two and Five blushed. None of the numbers dared tell the Wise Wizz of Woo what they'd been quarrelling about.

"Oh come on…" said the Wise Wizz of Woo. "You've disturbed me now you might as well tell me what's wrong."

"It's… It's like this," began Seven nervously. "We're just a bit bored of going in the same order all the time. We… we… were trying to agree on a different order to go in some of the time."

The numbers thought the Wise Wizz of Woo would be really angry after he'd spent so much time teaching the numbers the special order he'd made up for them. Most of the numbers covered their ears expecting him to shout at them. But he didn't. The Wise Wizz of Woo always liked it when people and numbers played around with maths ideas. It was one of the reasons maths had been invented as well as for it to be useful now and again.

"Well, well, well," he said. "Personally I think the order you go in at the moment is perfect but I'd love to hear your ideas. What have you come up with so far?"

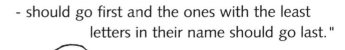

- should go first and the ones with the least letters in their name should go last."

"Another excellent idea!" said the Wise Wizz of Woo. "So what would be the new order this time?"

"Well, um..." began Three.

"We're going to need the help of children reading this story again aren't we?" asked the Wise Wizz of Woo.

"That's a great idea," agreed Three. "To be honest with you I couldn't quite remember how to spell some of the other numbers."

"Any more ideas?" asked the Wise Wizz of Woo.

"Well actually, Two and I were quarrelling over another idea," said One. "I think all the odd numbers should go first and then all the even numbers second but Two thinks it should be the other way around."

"I do!" said Two.

"That's kind of two excellent ideas at once," said the Wise Wizz of Woo. "Do either of you know the order the numbers would be in if we did it either of those ways?"

"Er..." said One.

"Um..." said Two.

"We're going to need some more help from the children reading this story aren't we?"

"Well…" began Four excitedly. "As I've got the most sticky out bits in the shape of my number I think I should go first and Three should go next because she's got three sticky out bits in the shape of her numbers and the numbers with no sticky out bits could go last."

"What an excellent idea!" said the Wise Wizz of Woo. "So what would be the new order of the numbers?"

"Well... I haven't actually worked that out yet properly," admitted Four.

"Perhaps we could get the children reading this story to work it out for us?" suggested the Wise Wizz of Woo.

"That's a great idea," agreed Four. "All the numbers were moving about so much while we were quarrelling I couldn't work it out."

"Who else had an idea?" asked the Wise Wizz of Woo.

"I did!" said Three. "I think that the numbers with the most letters in their name - like me

"Can we ask them to work the order out as well?" asked Six. "We don't seem to be very good at doing it ourselves."

"Good idea. Let's do that," said the Wise Wizz of Woo.

So they did.

To be read after children complete investigations

A little while later when the numbers and the Wise Wizz of Woo had listened to the orders you worked out and made up they were very impressed.

"Haven't they worked hard and been very clever," said Seven.

"They certainly have," said the Wise Wizz of Woo.

"I liked all of the orders," said Three.

"Me too!" said Two.

"ZZZZZ," said Eight. She was still asleep.

"How about we keep to the usual order most of the time but use all of the other orders for special occasions?" suggested the Wise Wizz of Woo.

"That's a great idea!!!" agreed all the numbers.

Except Eight because of course...

The End

"I think that's a great idea," agreed One. "I sometimes have a problem remembering which numbers are odd and which are even anyway."

"Me too!" said Two.

"Any more ideas?" asked the Wise Wizz of Woo.

No one said anything except Eight who said "ZZZZ" again which didn't really help.

"We've run out of ideas," said Five. "But it would be nice to see if we could think of some more."

"Perhaps we could ask the children reading this story to see if they can think of any more reasons for putting you in a different order?" suggested the Wise Wizz of Woo.

Ten's problem

Early Years Foundation Stage targets
By the end of the Early Years Foundation Stage, most children will be able to:

- say and use number names in order in familiar contexts
- count reliably up to 10 everyday objects
- recognise numerals 1 to 9
- talk about, recognise and recreate simple patterns
- use developing mathematical ideas and methods to solve practical problems

KS 1 Programme of Study
2a. count reliably up to 20 objects... be familiar with the numbers 11 to 20...

2b. create and describe number patterns...

Lesson plan

"How all the "teen" numbers are made using two columns."

"To decide what unit number Ten can go with to Twenty's party. "

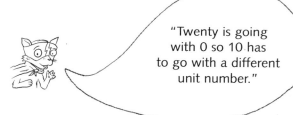

"Twenty is going with 0 so 10 has to go with a different unit number."

Read the first part of the story (the story is in two sections, the second section to be read after the children have thought about which number 10 could go with to the party.) You may want to join the 10 number card from the "How the numbers got their shape" story to each of the digit cards to illustrate the story as you go through it. This will help the children understand how to get started with their activities after listening to the story.

Having read the story explain that the children will be asked to think of reasons for a number 10 can pair up with to go to the party. You could remind them of the work they did in the problem solving lesson using the story "The Numbers have a Quarrel" or work they've done in other lessons. Ideally try not to give the children too many ideas, however, if appropriate you could suggest ideas such as seeing which number has the most "sticky out" bits, or which has most/least number of letters in its name or which is the highest/lowest odd/even number between 11 and 19.

The children could then work in pairs or in groups. Ask the children to construct all the numbers from 11 to 19 by joining each of the digits to a 10. Then ask them to match the resource strips with the names of the "teen" numbers on them with each number that they have made and glue the numbers and their names together. Ask them to arrange the numbers they've made in order. Some of them could go on display. After they have done this ask them to think about which "teen" number ten should go as to twenty's party and to then do a large drawing or painting of the number they think 10 should go to the party as and write/paint the name underneath. Then in front of a group/the class give a brief presentation which begins, "I think 10 should join up with __ to go to the party as ___ because...." Ask them to see if they can think of as many reasons as possible why 10 should go as the "teen" number they have chosen.

When the children have made their presentations, read the last part of the story explaining the Wise Wizz of Woo and 10's solution. Ask the children to express their opinion about whether they think any of their ideas/their friends' ideas are better than the Wise Wizz of Woo's ideas and explain why. Perhaps you could have a "vote" at the end for a particular number or idea.

Further ideas

You could discuss with a class or group how they could make a presentation for the Wise Wizz of Woo to show how doubling works – and what results you get when you double! Possibly some groups could show how tripling, quadrupling, going up in tens works.

Should any further ideas be needed, here are some we have thought of!

11/Eleven
Same number/digit in units column as tens column - which also makes the number symmetrical. (Though Ten might still be accused of favouritism!) Lowest odd

number. Number of players in a hockey team and a football team. The age when the children will leave junior school.

12/Twelve
Lowest even number. Makes a "dozen". Shortest word between 11-19. Only word with a W in it. The last number between 11-19 in the dictionary. The number of Apostles.

13/Thirteen
First "teen" word but some people think it's unlucky. Number of players in a rugby league team. The number in a "baker's dozen".

14/Fourteen
First "teen" number with the correct spelling of the units number. 4 is the number with the most "sticky out" bits, so of these numbers 14 will have the most number of "sticky out" bits.

15/Fifteen
15 is exactly in between 11 and 19 so it could be seen as the "fairest" choice for that reason. Number of players in a rugby union team. Shortest odd "teen" word.

16/Sixteen
Shortest "teen" word. Age when the children can ride a scooter/moped and buy a lottery ticket!!! (And used to be the age when they could leave school!)

17/Seventeen
Most number of letters in its name. It's got four e's in its name which is more than any of the other numbers. Age when you can drive a car.

18/Eighteen
Biggest even number and even number with the most letters in its name. (Eight is always asleep in the other stories so perhaps she'll be asleep again so Ten can't take her! Unless he/she can carry her to the party!) 8 is the number with no "sticky out" bits. Only "gh" word. Age when children become adults. First number between 11-19 in the dictionary.

19/Nineteen
Biggest number between 11-19. Biggest odd number. Only word which starts with an n (there are two of each other beginning letters.)

Resources

Per Pair or group. One set of the number cards provided with "How the Wise Wizz of Woo invented numbers" story (see page 10). You will need to make several copies of the 10 which could be copied en mass separately. Nine 10's needed altogether.

Teen number name cards. (Resource provided with this story.)

Glue e.g. glue sticks.

Resources for drawing or painting a large teen number and its name.

Eleven
Twelve
Thirteen
Fourteen
Fifteen
Sixteen
Seventeen
Eighteen
Nineteen

Ten went to see the Wise Wizz of Woo because he had a problem. Maths hadn't been invented for long and the Wise Wizz of Woo was trying to work out how doubling worked. When Ten arrived he put down the two sets of counters he was working with and turned to listen to Ten.

"I've got a problem," explained Ten.

"So have I, this doubling isn't as easy as I thought it would be," said the Wise Wizz of Woo. "Maybe you can help me with it later, I can't work out if the double of two is seven or four… but anyway, let's deal with your problem first. What is it?"

"Well as you know it's Twenty's birthday next week," began Ten.

"I certainly do," agreed the Wise Wizz of Woo. "Everyone in the Land of Numbers is looking forward to going to it."

"So am I," said Ten. "But my problem is I don't know which number to go as. You see I can't go as just Ten because of course Twenty will be taking Zero with him to be Twenty."

"I see," said the Wise Wizz of Woo who could see what Ten's problem

was now. "Well why don't you go with One and be Eleven?" he asked.

"Well, I'd quite like to but I know the other numbers will complain because then I'll be the same number in the units column as the tens column and they'll say I'm showing favouritism," said Ten.

"Hmm," hmmed the Wise Wizz of Woo. This was turning out to be more difficult than doubling things. "Well why not go with Two and go as Twelve."

"Well, I wouldn't mind that either but then the other numbers will complain that I'm only going with Twelve because Twelve is also a special number called a Dozen," replied Ten.

"I see…" said the Wise Wizz of Woo. What he could see was that he was going to have to teach the numbers to work better together, without being so fussy about which number was doing what.

"I can't go with Three and be Thirteen because some of the numbers say that Thirteen is unlucky and that if I did we might bring bad luck to Twenty's party." continued Ten.

The Wise Wizz of Woo thought it was crazy to think of a number being unlucky so he just hmmed again and let Ten carry on.

"I can't actually go with Four to be Fourteen or Five to be Fifteen anyway because they're serving the drinks and the food behind the bar." continued Ten. "I can't go with Six to be Sixteen or Seven to be Seventeen because Six and Seven are singing songs on stage for Twenty. I can't

go with Eight to be Eighteen because Eight'll be asleep as usual...."

The Wise Wizz of Woo laughed. Eight was always falling asleep (or thinking about breakfast if she was awake!)

"What about going with Nine then to be Nineteen?" asked the Wise Wizz of Woo.

To be read after children complete investigations

When they'd heard all your ideas, the Wise Wizz of Woo and Ten looked at each other.

"What brilliant ideas," said Ten.
"Yes, thank you children," said the Wise Wizz of Woo. "Sorry about that screaming in the first part of the story by the way. I hope I didn't scare you. Anyway we'll tell our idea and then you can decide which of the ideas you like best, ours or one of yours."

"Our idea," said Ten. "Is that I could be different numbers during the party. I could go with One to be Eleven but after a while I could team up with Two and be Twelve. Then I could be with Three and be Thirteen. I sure it won't be unlucky if I'm only Thirteen for a while. Then when most people have eaten and drunk as much as they want I could team up with Four and then Five behind the bar to

"Well, if I do that all the other numbers will complain that I'm going as the highest number I can be and not going with them because they're not so high."

The Wise Wizz of Woo wanted to scream. So he did.

"I'm going to have a word with the numbers after Twenty's party!!!" he screamed. "But in the meantime..." he said calming down. "I've got a good idea. Let's see if we can get the children reading this story to think of any ideas about who you should go as? Meanwhile we'll see if we can come up with an idea as well."

"That's a great idea," said Ten. "Let's do it." So they did.

be Fourteen and Fifteen. Then I could team up with Six to be Sixteen while Seven sings a solo and Seven to be Seventeen while Six sings a solo. By that time Eight will have woken up so I can team up with her to be Eighteen and finally I can team up with Nine to be Nineteen."

"So now it's up to you children. Whatever you decide we'll do. Thanks for your help, we'll see you in the next story!" said the Wizz Wizz of Woo waving at you.

"Yes...BYE!!!" said Ten waving as well.

"Now then," said the Wise Wizz of Woo, turning back to his work bench, as we were leaving the story. "I think I've worked out what double two is but what's three doubled... two or six?... hmm..."

The End

Early Years Foundation Stage targets

By the end of the Early Years Foundation Stage, most children will be able to:

- in practical activities and discussion begin to use the vocabulary involved in adding and subtracting.
- Begin to relate addition to combining two groups of objects, and subtraction to "taking away".

KS 1 Programme of Study

Ma2. 3a. understand addition and use related vocabulary: recognise that addition can be done in any order: understand subtraction as both "take away" and "difference" and use related vocabulary; recognise that subtraction is the inverse of addition…

Lesson plan

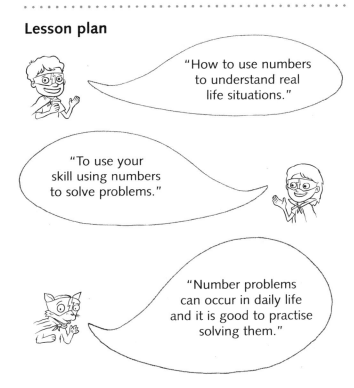

"How to use numbers to understand real life situations."

"To use your skill using numbers to solve problems."

"Number problems can occur in daily life and it is good to practise solving them."

The story gives the children the opportunity to carry out problem solving using addition and subtraction in various ways. As one resource we have provided cartoons of the different bands (before they split up and become new bands!) and the different nationality teams climbing up Mount Everest (and then playing each other at football!) These could be used along with the worksheets provided to allow the children to separate the band members or climbing teams to work out how many people there would be in each new band or climbing team/football team. The figures could be used as a way of recording the new combinations for the children's own records or a display, to enhance by writing down significant information about each new combination, for example if it's a new band, what their name is and which bands the members came from or if it's the climbers, why and when they have combined together – to climb or play football. They could do a "before and after" picture, e.g. showing where the band members came from. This could be a way of showing conservation of number.

The work could be differentiated by allowing more able children to attempt solving the questions on the question sheets using their own methods whilst guiding less able students using one particular method, e.g. cutting out the cartoon figures and putting them together to make the new groups.

In a class discussion following the activity, the children could discuss and explain how they worked out the answers to the various problems. As an extension activity you could ask the children as a class, or in groups to think of different possible combinations and present and explain them to the rest of the class.

Resources

Cartoons of the original bands and of the original climbing teams.

Gimme Five (boy band)
Flirty Four (girl band)
Soul 7
One-Hit Wanda
Three's a crowd (boy/girl band)

2 man British team
4-strong French team
3-women American team
5-strong Russian team
3-strong Bulgarian team
6-strong Greek team

Worksheets.

Possibly also, scissors, glue, pens/pencils backing paper for the children's own records or class display.

Gimme Five

Flirty Four

Soul 7

One-Hit Wanda

Three's a crowd

2 man British team

4-strong French team

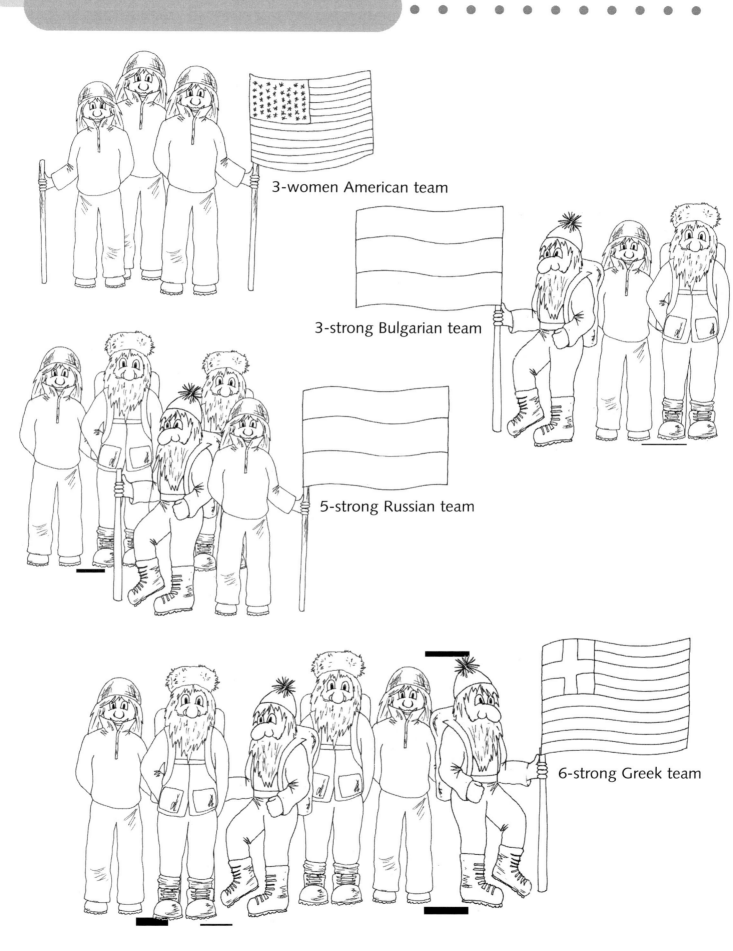

3-women American team

3-strong Bulgarian team

5-strong Russian team

6-strong Greek team

Name: _____

Listen to the story again and see if you can answer these questions.

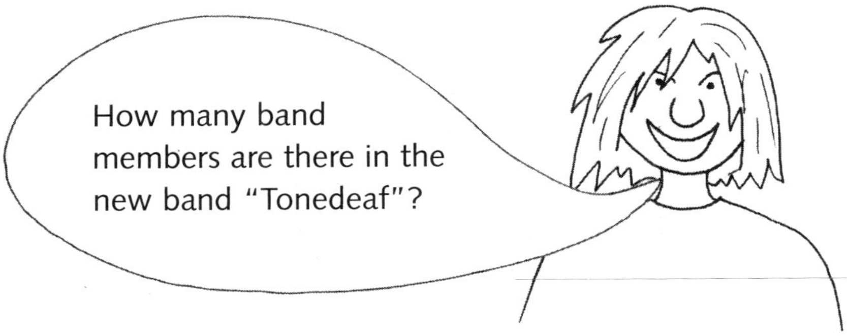

How many band members are there in the new band "Tonedeaf"?

_____

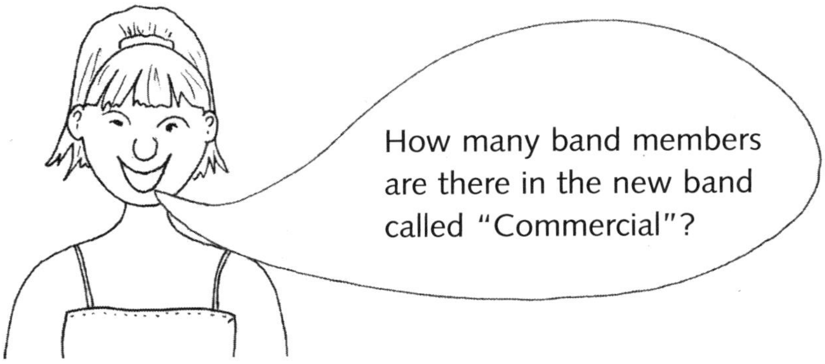

How many band members are there in the new band called "Commercial"?

_____

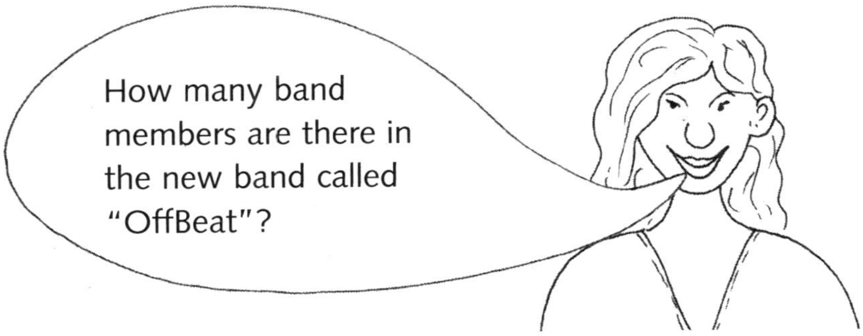

How many band members are there in the new band called "OffBeat"?

_____

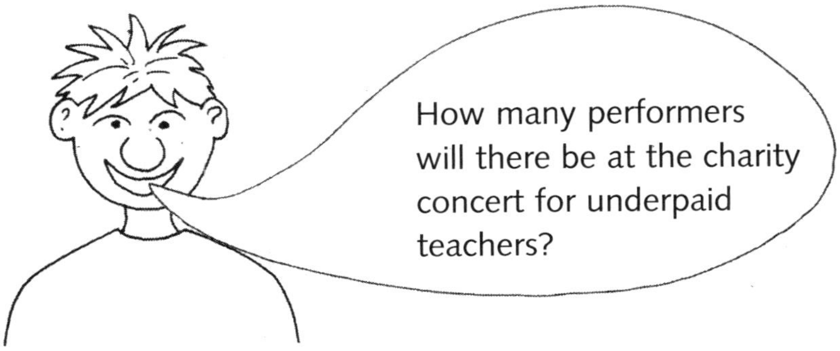

How many performers will there be at the charity concert for underpaid teachers?

_____

Worksheet 2: Climb every mountain

Name: ____________________

Listen to the story again and see if you can answer these questions.

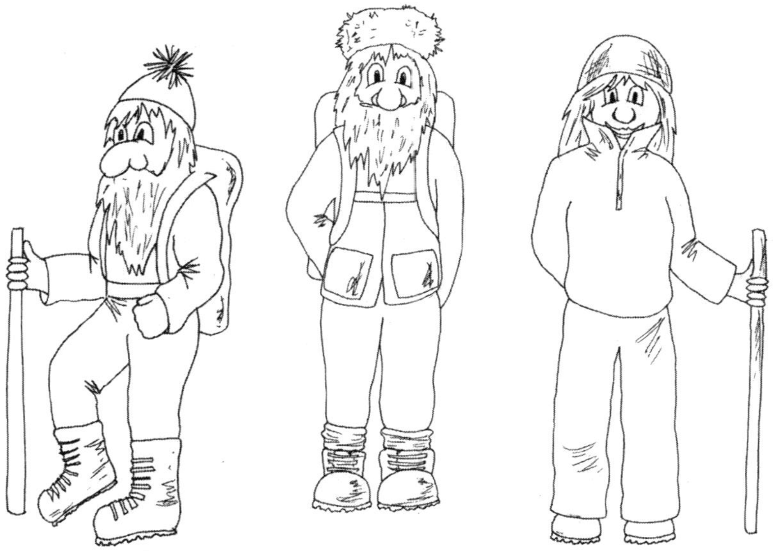

How many climbers will there be when the British team and French team join the American team?

____

How many climbers will there be when the Russian team and Bulgarian team join the Greek team?

____

How many climbers will reach the top of Mount Everest altogether?

____

How many in the British, French and Greek football team?

____

How many in the American, Russian and Bulgarian football team?

____

Hello if you've just joined us on 24/7 News. The headlines tonight. The Prime Minister made a speech on National Exciting Maths Day. She said that she liked maths stating that she couldn't take anything away from subtraction and in addition to that she loved addition.

Now on the 24/7 News it's over to Celina with the latest pop celebrity news and gossip…

Thank you Michael. Well it's been quite a week in the pop celebrity world. Argumentative boy band "Gimme Five" finally split up, after an even worse argument than usual with two of the band, joining the all-girl band "Flirty Four" to form new band "ToneDeaf". Not to be left out frozen in the pop world hinterland, the remaining members of "Gimme Five" have decided to collaborate with other musicians to produce a special album celebrating the last fifty years of piped music. They'll be joining four members of soul band "Soul 7", who have also just split up and paparazzi idol "One-Hit Wanda", who curiously now has three top ten hits under her belt. (Admittedly it's a very thin belt.) This eclectic mix of musicians has decided to name themselves "Commercial" while they work together.

The remaining three members of "Soul 7", blaming the other four for the split and not their disgusting eating habits, have teamed up with girl-boy band "Three's a crowd" to form the new band "OffBeat". Their forthcoming album should be out on the 4th next month.

Still artistic temperaments and musical differences will be put aside later this month as all the performers are teaming up to play at a charity concert in aid of underpaid teachers. Back to you Michael…

Thank you Celina. It's about time someone did something about teachers…

Anyway we're just getting news about the latest situation affecting mountaineering teams from different countries trying to climb Mount Everest at the moment.

Apparently the conditions have become very harsh, and we hear that the two man British team have been helped by the four-strong French team, all of whom have decided to join the American team made up of three women. Meanwhile in a dramatic rescue the five-strong Russian team were helped out of trouble by the three-strong Bulgarian team. They have now caught up with the Greek expedition, consisting of six mountaineers. This new group expects to catch up with the Anglo-French-American team in the next day or so, so that all the mountaineers are likely to reach the summit at about the same time! We've heard already that when the

mountaineers get back to base camp they're planning a football match to celebrate this unusual and historic event, between one team consisting of the British, French and Greek mountaineers playing against an American, Russian and Bulgarian team. Here at 24/7 news we can't wait to hear which team of mountaineers turns out to be the "tops"! Ho ho.

Now it's 9.00 and way past our bedtime, so hope you'll join us tomorrow when we're on your screens again at 10.00. Thank you for watching 24/7 News.

Goodnight

Bernice the Octopus buys a watch

KS 1. Programme of Study
Ma 2. 1a. approach problems involving number, and data presented in a variety of forms, in order to identify what they need to do.

Ma 2. 1b. develop flexible approaches to problem solving and look for ways to overcome difficulties.

Ma2. 2b. create and describe number patterns... recognise sequences...

Ma2. 4a choose sensible calculation methods to solve whole-number problems (including problems involving... measures)...

Ma 3. 4a Pupils should be taught to... put familiar events in chronological order... compare the durations of events using a standard unit of time.

Factoid

Octopi actually have three hearts, a main heart responsible for the main pumping of the blood and two "brachial" hearts to give the blood and extra boost of pressure when it passes through them. (Hence the joke about Bernice not having "the three hearts" to tell Sid she doesn't like the first heart he shows her.)

Lesson plan

"To solve problems using ordinal numbers, the numbers used to put things in order."

"To think about and discuss problems using ordinal numbers and time."

The story provides an opportunity for the children to practice using ordinal numbers, to work out some simple problems relating to time and to carry out an investigation. The idea behind the investigation is introduced when Cameron Crayfish suggests that Bernice's fourth tentacle is her middle tentacle. So the children could be asked to investigate whether the fourth object in a group of eight is actually the

middle object. They could also be asked to see if there are any patterns to do with the middle numbers of different numbers of objects. (Even numbers of things don't actually have a middle object but odd numbers do.) Different groups could think of different ways of exploring this problem and finding some way to present their ideas to the rest of the class.

As Carl the Crab asks awkward questions in the story, namely "What tentacle are you going to wear your watch on?" and "Which is your eighth tentacle?" you could first ask the children for their thoughts/ideas about these problems before Bernice attempts to find her own solutions.

As a class or in groups, you could ask the children how much time Bernice has between her various appointments, possibly with some children asking them to draw these times on pictures of clocks. Her various appointments are;

10.00 Report on sea weed survey
11.30 Coral Council Crustacean Consortium
1.00   Lunch
2.00   Shark Seminar
3.15   Meeting with Finance Fish
(Also she gets to Sid the Seahorse's jewellery shell at 9.30 and leaves ten minutes later with her "Porpoise" watch.)

Further work

You could ask the children to imagine a creature with 20 tentacles - which tentacle could that creature wear its watch on? You could ask the children to go as far as they can using ordinal numbers, or use ordinals jumping up in twos, tens etc.

You could ask the children to see if they can find out about why the number six is so strongly linked with the ways we measure time. (It has to do with the fact that the Sumerians and Babylonians counted in 60's.) They could also investigate why six is called "half a dozen."

You could ask the children to find out what oceans the "Seven Seas" are and what and where the seven continents are.

Finally you could say that Bernice has to go to a business meeting with a shark who hates to see animals wearing more than one watch. Bernice is back to her original problem. Which of the animal's ideas did the children think was best and/or can they think of a better time related reason why she should wear her watch on a particular tentacle?

Bernice the Octopus buys a watch

Bernice the Octopus was an ambitious executive. She worked for the coral council and had to attend meetings all around the sea-bed making sure all the underwater creatures were receiving all the services they required, making sure they were up to date with their council tax and so on. Why on this very day she had a meeting at 10.00 to report about the seaweed survey, then at 11.30 she had to be back at the coral council caves to attend a crustacean consortium. After lunch at 1.00 she then had to go to a shark seminar that was scheduled for 2.00 and finally at 3.15 she needed to fly (well swim quickly) to see the Finance Fish to go over this February's facts and figures.

This was why Bernice needed at watch. So our story begins with Bernice visiting Sid the Seahorse in his jewellery shell at 9.30 in the morning.

"How did you manage before?" asked Sid, knowing how busy Bernice was all the time.

"I had a seal secretary before to tell me when I had to go to my next appointment but when we looked at the last council budget we realised we couldn't shell out for seal secretaries any more and so we had to let him go," Bernice replied.

"That's council's for you the world under, not shelling out for staff," sighed Sid, not fully realising just how completely true that was the whole world over as well. "Anyway, I've got this lovely "Bubble" watch; it's very hard wearing, why it even works in air!"

Bernice didn't have the three hearts to tell Sid that she didn't really like it; she thought the strap was decorated with far too many garishly large pearls, it just made the watch look quite gauche. Give her a few small pebbles anytime, they were far more elegant.

Sensing the watch he has suggested hadn't got Bernice's beak buzzing, Sid brought forward a smaller watch. "Now this one is a beauty," he said. "As you can see it's quite petite but very pretty. It's one of those "designer" "Porpoise" watches… you've probably seen the adverts… "Designed for a purpose by porpoises… and the purpose is perfect precision." Personally I think they are perfect and this one has kept perfect time ever since it's been up on the shelf in my shell. They're such good watches and such good value; I've ordered several more for my shell to sell in a sale. I'll sell you this one at sale price, if you like."

Bernice couldn't help agreeing that it was a lovely watch and very good value. A pretty petite "Porpoise" watch like that couldn't help giving you more poise and was indeed perfect for a person in her position.

Ten minutes later Bernice was swimming out of Sid's shell, holding her watch proudly before her. As it happened Carl the Crab was just crawling sideways by.

"Wow", is that one of the "Porpoise" watches?" Carl asked his friend. "Wow, like, they're so wet and salty man!" (Carl was a bit of a hippy and often used these outdated expressions. Nowadays the kids

were calling everything "like wavy" or "oceanic man.")

"Well it is rather petite and pretty…" replied Bernice blushing brightly.

"Which tentacle are you going to wear it on?" Carl asked, not realising that he had just asked a question that would cause much confusion and concern.

"Er… um…" er and ummed Bernice. She hadn't thought about that up until now. "I don't know. Oh sorry…" she said looking at her watch. "Got to go, I've got to get to my seaweed survey meeting at ten o'clock and it's about a seven minute swim. See you sideling along sideways sometime! Bye!"

"No worries, stay like buoyant man. Hope you decide what tentacle to use…" called Carl as Bernice swam into the distance. He shuffled off sideways to search for some shrimps for his supper. Neither he nor the shrimps would be going to the crustacean convention later on, despite being crustaceans. Still, that was politics for you. As Carl always said, "Politics is like an oil slick man… something you don't want to be in and which sucks the life out of you man…"

As it happened the details of the seaweed survey were soon sorted and reported so Bernice explained her problem to the other creatures at the meeting. She still had to hold her watch in her tentacles as she couldn't decide which tentacle to wear it on.

"Why don't you wear it on your first tentacle?" suggested Carlos Cod. "… As it's your first watch. Such a shame about the seal secretaries…"

"Or you could wear it on your second tentacle," said Sabina Squid as your watch has a "second" hand counting the seconds!"

"That's a good idea," said Evelyn Eel "Though it is a bit confusing because although that hand is called the second hand, it's only called the second hand because it counts the seconds. The first proper hand measures the hours, the real second hand measures the minutes and the third hand, called the "second" hand measures the seconds. So perhaps you should wear your new watch… which is lovely by the way… on your third tentacle… … or maybe that idea doesn't work at all… sorry." Evelyn did have a tendency to

notice problems with ideas and then come up with more confusing solutions.

"Well thank you for your input," said Bernice, who was rapidly being put off wearing a watch at all because of this unexpected tentacle dilemma that Carl had created. If he hadn't said anything, I would have just put it on one of my tentacles without thinking, she thought to herself. Then, noticing the time on her new watch, she said to her friends, "Unfortunately I need to swim off now to get to the crustacean convention. Bye. See you swimming by sometime."

So Bernice swam off to the crustacean convention. Many crustaceans were at the convention, including several crabs and shrimp, despite Carl and his supper not being there. There were also other non-crustacean sea-creatures present, such as Bernice, who were attending the convention to show solidarity for crustaceans. Bernice found herself talking to a consortium of important crustaceans, including Cameron Crayfish, who was on secondment from a freshwater river in Devon. After discussing crustacean related issues, conversation turned to Bernice's problem with her watch.

"Half of eight is four, so wouldn't that make your fourth tentacle your middle tentacle? Why not wear it on that tentacle?" asked Cameron.

Cameron's question caused quite a commotion among the crustaceans because not all of them agreed that Bernice's fourth tentacle would be her middle tentacle. Bernice wasn't sure about that idea either because of this conundrum.

"Obviously if it was me, I would wear it on my fifth arm," said Stella the Starfish, another non-crustacean at the convention. "As we're unusual in having five arms, maybe you could wear it on your fifth tentacle to show your solidarity with starfish?"

Bernice quite liked that idea, she was quite a fan of starfish but she didn't want to upset any other type of sea-creature by showing favouritism, something that someone in her position certainly couldn't do. Also not all the starfish had five arms anyway.

"I think, you should wear your admirable timepiece on your sixth tentacle…," began Loraine Lobster contributing a suggestion. Loraine was well known for really enjoying mathematics, so Bernice was sure her idea would have something to do with maths and that it might well be the cleverest but most complicated suggestion so far. Her intuition proved to be spot on target as usual. "…

My reason for this suggestion being that the number six has such a strong connection with the measurement of time…" (Here we go thought Bernice.) "For you see as there are sixty seconds in a minute and sixty minutes in an hour, that means there are six lots of ten seconds in a minute and six lots of ten minutes in an hour. Each day is divided into 24 hours and four lots of six are 24, each year is divided into 12 months, so a year could be divided into two lots of six months, with six months being half of a year…"

There was silence around their little gathering for a while but then Scarlet Scampi voiced the thoughts of most of the other animals in their little group. "Um, I'm sorry Lorraine; you lost me on that bit about it being an admirable timepiece…"

Bernice didn't think she'd be using Lorraine's idea. She had visions of trying to explain it to Carl or any other of the creatures she might meet who'd known about her watch-wearing dilemma. As it happened it was time for her to swim off for a quick lunch before shooting off to the shark seminar, so she politely made her excuses and left, leaving Lorraine patiently explaining to Scarlet and the others that a "timepiece" was another term for a watch and doing her best to get back to explaining how the number six was so strongly linked with measuring time.

Shirley the Hammerhead Shark had an idea that Bernice quite liked when they were having a short snack after the shark seminar. "Why don't you wear it on your seventh tentacle?" Shirley asked. "As we often talk about the "seven seas" (or oceans really) that we sea creatures swim in. Funnily enough there are also seven continents that we swim around as well, so that matches with the idea too."

"What about the real seas, like the Mediterranean, and the Arabian Sea, they've not covered by the "seven seas" label and lots of us swim in them," said Tim the Tiger Shark, who'd been ear wigging their conversation. "Also there are lots of islands that aren't a part of the seven continents of the world but loads of us live in the waters around them."

"Ugun…" was all Bernice could say in reply to this because she didn't quite know how to respond to Tim's objections to Shirley's idea. She still quite liked the seven idea as it did cover most of the water they all lived in and most of the land they swam around. Fortunately it was time for her to go and see the Finance Fish to present her February report, so she left Shirley and Tim to battle it out between them.

The Finance Fish was pleased with February's figures and – as she was so good with figures – Bernice asked for her help in figuring out her problem. "Well, probably because I always like to see figures that are as large as possible, I would have to suggest that you wear your watch on your eighth tentacle. I know Stella the Starfish is proud of being a starfish and her idea of you showing solidarity with starfish was clever, however I think you should be proud of having eight tentacles and of being an octopus. Everyone should be proud of who they are."

It was nearly time to swim home to her cave, so Bernice thanked the Finance Fish for her suggestion, wrote up the days report (using her own ink) and began swimming home. By a remarkable co-incidence she came across Carl, who was licking his pincers, having just enjoyed his shrimp supper.

"Hey that's like ripply man," said Carl. "I was just wondering if you'd decided which tentacle to wear your watch on."

Bernice described the different ideas that had been suggested to her during the day (Carl wasn't sure if her fourth tentacle was her middle tentacle either) and told him that she'd decided to wear her watch on her eighth tentacle as the Finance Fish had suggested.

"Wow, that's like really clear and unpolluted man," said Carl enthusiastically. "I'm so glad you sorted that out. Um… if you don't mind me asking, which one of your tentacles is your eighth tentacle?"

Bernice blinked at Carl. Then she turned the tips of all her tentacles towards her.

She looked at all her tentacles but couldn't decide which one of them was her eighth tentacle. To be honest she couldn't decide which number any of her tentacles were, she'd never thought of her tentacles as being numbered until today, they'd always just been her tentacles and she'd just got on with using them when and where needed. She decided the best thing to do right now was scream and that the second best thing to do was go and have a lie down in her cave.

"AAAAAAAAGH!!" Bernice screamed as she disappeared over the ridge of the reef. "Hey, like choppy man, I hope I didn't say anything to upset you," said Carl in the general direction of Bernice's disappearing figure. "That would be like turbulent man..." and he sidled off sadly sideways.

Happily the time came for this tale to have a happy ending. About a week later Carl was crawling across the coral, trying to creep up on some crunchy crustaceans for breakfast when Bernice swam into view, looking a lot happier than she had done the last time he'd seen her.

"Hey, like blue-green man. How are you?" asked Carl. "Did you decide which tentacle was your eighth tentacle in the end?"

"Actually I wasn't able to decide which tentacle was which," Bernice replied.

"Oh, like stormy man... you're not going to start screaming again are you?" asked Carl.

"Oh no," Bernice continued, smiling at her friends concern. "I found a different solution to my problem. I remembered Sid saying he was going to be selling his watches at sale price and I realised that as an executive I have to phone up other executives around the world from time to time. I did a deal with Sid and bought another seven watches at a special price, so now I'm wearing a watch on every tentacle and I know the time in Sydney, Tokyo, Hong Kong, Cairo, London, New York, Rio de Janeiro and Los Angeles! Sorry got to go, going to a lecture about lungfish. Bye!"

"Bye!" called Carl to Bernice's once more disappearing figure. "Well, that really is just tropical man."

The End

All shapes and sizes

Early Years Foundation Stage targets
By the end of the Early Years Foundation Stage, most children   will be able to:

• use language such as "circle" or "bigger" to describe the shape and size of solids and flat shapes.

KS 1 Programme of Study
Ma 3. 2a Pupils should be taught to describe properties of shapes that they can see or visualise using the related vocabulary.

Ma 3. 2b observe, handle and describe common… 3D shapes, name and describe the mathematical features of common.. 3D shapes, including… cubes, cuboids, then… cylinders, pyramids, cones and spheres.

Ma 3. 2c. create… 3D shapes.

Ma 3. 3a observe, visualise and describe… movements using common words.

Ma 3. 3c. recognise right angles.

Lesson plan

"About many of the names and features of solid shapes."

"To investigate some of the features of solid shapes."

"All solid shapes have different features and we need to learn what they are."

Having read the story, the children could explore the features of solid shapes introduced by the story. If you are able to provide the children with plenty of the shapes (and they could survive the occasional tumble!) you could ask the children to play "stacking", the game King Cube used to play when a boy, where the shapes try to build a shape that's as high and wide as they can make. Ask the children to investigate, then discuss and record, the features of the different shapes that affect how well they can play "stacking" (for example some will be able to balance on the top of the stack but will not be very good at supporting other shapes on top of them, so they may vary from being "brilliant" at playing stacking to being "rubbish".)

Another investigation could entail the children investigating the different ways that the shapes can move including thinking about how they could change direction. In the story it talks about how King Cube has to make quarter/right-angle turns to move about, and also how cones, cylinders and spheres can roll around in different ways. Once again the children could then discuss and record their findings.

As an extension activity one child, or group, could give instructions to another to move a shape from one location to another. (The group describing the movement could have decided – or been told – where they want the shape to go but the group moving the shape are not, so that the first group have to successfully describe how they want the shape moved!)

The story also discusses how King Cube has to make quarter turns; also described as right angle turns. The children could be provided with – or make – a "Right Angle finder", which could simply be the corner of a piece of card. They then have to find as many right angles as possible in the classroom. They could also be asked to record which shapes have to turn through right angles and which have to make turns of other angles, e.g. a triangular prism.

If you are able to provide the children with nets of shapes printed on paper or card they could draw faces (or crowns!) on the faces of the various sides as a way of investigating the number of different faces on the shapes. (Making the shapes into nets could be a way of providing suitable shapes for playing "Stacking"!

Further activities

You could ask the children to see if they can make up the joke about the triangles that is referred to several times in the story but never told!

A good dram warm up exercise is to split the children into groups of about 5/6 and then secretly tell them the name of a solid shape. They then have to work out how to demonstrate this shape and see if the rest of the class can guess what shape they are. (NB A rule of the game is that the children are not allowed to climb on each other!)

Resources

Solid shapes, ideally ones that can be drawn on.

Nets of shapes that can be examined and made into solid shapes.

A "Right Angle finder" – a right angle, possibly the corner of a piece of card!

All shapes and sizes

Once upon a time there was a magical kingdom called the Land of Meringue. I don't know why it was called the Land of Meringue, it just was. Don't blame me, I'm just the storyteller. Everybody who lived in the Land of Meringue was a solid shape.

One day a new king was crowned called King Cube. Now King Cube was really a very pleasant shape except that he had a serious problem, which he'd kept secret until he was crowned.

King Cube didn't like spheres.

How crazy is that? It's like one kind of person not liking another kind of person, which is also crazy. As you'll see King Cube learned his lesson in the end. All shapes (and people of course) are special in their own unique way.

One reason King Cube thought he didn't like spheres had to do with a game the shapes used to play when they were little girl and boy shapes at school, called "Stacking". In

this game the shapes would line up next to each other or balance on top of each other and see how high and wide a shape they could make altogether.

As all the cubes, like Prince Cube, had flat square sides, they were brilliant at playing "Stacking" because any shape could stack on top of them perfectly. All the other shapes could join in the game in some way or another to become part of the stack; all the shapes apart from the spheres that is.

Of course nothing could be stacked on top of a sphere and the spheres would roll off whatever shape they were stacked on top of. Most of the other shapes didn't mind about this - in fact they thought it was really funny - but King Cube had found it really annoying.

Another thing he found annoying about spheres was that they could roll about everywhere so quickly because they didn't have any sides, corners or edges, to slow them down, like he did. He had to do a whole quarter turn to move in any direction, one turn at a time. It didn't matter that each turn had a posh name, called a right angle turn; it still took him ages to get anywhere.

King Cube wasn't completely keen on cones because they could roll around so easily on one of their sides so well, even though they could only go round and round in circles. When he saw cylinders rolling too and fro quickly like they could that annoyed him but the spheres rolling around so fast in any direction they wanted to go REALLY DROVE HIM NUTS!!!!.

Only King Cube wasn't sad that all the spheres had gone. But he was sad. He didn't like all the shapes in his land being unhappy. He decided to cheer everyone up by entertaining them by becoming a "Comic King Cube" for the evening and sharing a huge banquet with them afterwards.

One morning he decided he'd had enough of the spheres and being King he thought he could do what he liked, "I WANT THOSE SPHERES ROLLED OUT OF MY KINGDOM RIGHT NOW, IF NOT SOONER!!!" he shouted to his guards.

The King's guards, Sergeant Cylinder, Corporal Cone and Private Pyramid were very unhappy as they liked all the spheres they'd met but they did as they were told because soldiers are good at doing that.

In one corner of Meringue was a very steep hill on the other side of which was somewhere that wasn't a part of the Land of Meringue. The unhappy guards took the spheres to the top of the hill and rolled them down the other side.

"We'll never see our friends again," thought the guards and cried in that heart-wrenching way that only shapes can. The whole of Meringue became a much sadder place without the spheres rolling around joyfully everywhere.

"Ha!" he thought to himself, "Once all the shapes have laughed until their corners ache watching my comedy act and once everyone's enjoyed the banquet, they'll have all forgotten about those silly spheres and they'll cheer up again!" The Chef at the castle was a cuboid and so everyone called her the "Cook Cuboid".

She was a brilliant cook and she knew that under normal circumstances all the shapes would enjoy the banquet King Cube asked her to prepare. She was quite a wise shape and didn't think the shapes would enjoy the evening King Cube had prepared for them as much as he thought they would.

Well all the shapes crowded into the courtyard of King Cube's castle and King Cube told them the jokes he had made up. At any other time the King's jokes would have seemed really funny; despite being a nit-wit of a king, King Cube was a good comedian but none of the shapes were in the mood for laughing and didn't laugh once, not even at the joke about the triangles, which King Cube thought was his best joke.

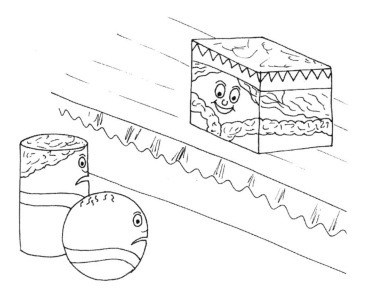

eating. The Cook Cuboid had made a lot of delicious food for everybody.

Now shapes can put on weight quite quickly and slowly, as he stuffed himself with more and more food, the King began to change shape... His sides started to bulge outwards. His straight edges and sharp corners started to look less and less like straight edges and sharp corners. The straight edges began to curve outwards and the sharp corners gradually disappeared...

Just as King Cube was stuffing the last crumbs into his mouth, Sergeant Cylinder looked into the kitchen on his nightly round making sure everyone was behaving themselves.

"Leave me alone, you miserable shapes!" shouted King Cube rudely, not even noticing that Sergeant Cylinder was on his own, when he heard the kitchen door open.

"'Ello, 'Ello, 'Ello... what have we got here then?" asked Sergeant Cylinder in that special

"Oh! I don't care!" declared King Cube after yet another embarrassing silence after he'd finished telling a joke (even though he did). "Go home and be miserable - see if I care!" (So they did and he still cared.)

King Cube irritably turned over and over through tediously slow right angles until he got to the kitchen, where he sat by the fire to cheer himself up.

Sitting by the fire didn't cheer the King up very much but looking up the King could see that the kitchen table was piled high with the delicious food he'd asked the Cook Cuboid to prepare for the banquet. Since none of the shapes had bothered to laugh at any of his jokes – not even the joke about the triangles – he didn't see why he should share it with his shapes any more.

"Hmm…" thought King Cube. "Yum... Yum....."

So he started eating... and he carried on eating... and eating... and eating… and

you-are-probably-in-big-trouble-now-I've-seen-you voice that sergeants use when someone is probably in big trouble.

"What are you talking about?" demanded King Cube, not realising that he was now in very big trouble and he made it worse by adding, "Can't you see I'm the King, you stupid shape???"

"The King, eh?" said the Sergeant Cylinder, this time sounding very calm and thoughtful and pretending not to notice that he had just been called "stupid." Any soldier will tell you that when a sergeant becomes very calm and thoughtful in the way that he talks to you that you are in such deep deep trouble you might as well help dig the hole. "The King my lad is a cube..." Sergeant Cylinder continued, calmly, "You know... six lovely flat square sides... eight sharp corners... and TWELVE (TWELVE!) bea-utiful straight edges... now you my lad are a... sphere... without a single straight edge, a single sharp corner or even one flat square side... because-you-are-a-sphere... and the King ordered us to roll you spheres out of his kingdom this morning. Not that we wanted to roll the other spheres out of the kingdom... though in your case..."

"What on earth are you talking abou... abou... abou..." replied the King, who had just seen himself reflected in the kitchen saucepans. "I... I... I'm a sphere!"

"Yes sir... how clever of you to realise," said the Sergeant Cylinder, wondering how it was possible for any shape not to know what shape it was. For a moment he almost felt sorry for this silly sphere... but only for a moment, he was a sergeant after all.

"B... B... But..." said King Cube, trying to explain. He was so confused and flustered all he could say was, "B... B... But..." as the Sergeant Cylinder rolled him up and then down the hill, on the other side of which was somewhere that wasn't a part of the Land of Meringue.

Guess what King Cube found when he finished rolling down the hill... apart from the bottom of the hill, silly! All the other spheres that didn't used to be kings!

"B... B... But I'm the King!" shouted King Cube, finally finishing his sentence.

"No you're not... you're a sphere, just like we are, what are you talking about?" asked all the other spheres.

"Oh no! Let's not go through all that again!" said King Cube and he explained what had happened.

Well even though he'd had them rolled out of his kingdom the spheres were very forgiving shapes and they all felt sorry for King Cube.

"Well, there's only one thing for you to do," said one of the spheres. "You're going to have to go on a diet and become a cube again. But before you do, I think you should find out what it's like to be a sphere!"

"YES!!" agreed all the other spheres.

The spheres rolled into King Cube to make him roll until he got the hang of rolling about on his own. Soon King Cube was having a whale of a time whizzing about.

"WHEEE!!" he shouted as he rolled in one direction.

"WOWWW!!" he shouted as he rolled in another.

King Cube saw how silly he had been to throw such fun shapes as spheres out of his kingdom and felt very very guilty.

"I'm a fool, that's what I am," said King Cube.

"Yes," said the spheres kindly but truthfully.

Luckily it doesn't take long for shapes to lose weight and so, only a week later, King Cube turned over and over though quarter (right angle) turns until he was back in his kingdom, followed by all the spheres rolling merrily along behind him.

The rest of the shapes from Meringue were DELIGHTED to see them all and rolled over or turned over excitedly.

"LET'S HAVE A PARTY IN MY CASTLE!!!!!" shouted King Cube.

"YES!!!" shouted all the other shapes.

So they did.

The End

No it's not... Not quite anyway. The King decided that as he'd made such a mess of being a king he'd be a comedian instead and toured the land telling his jokes. (Everyone found them funny now – especially the joke about the triangles!) As she was so wise, the Land of Meringue came to be ruled by the former Cook Cuboid; though she now became Queen Cuboid. She ruled alongside her daughter Princess Prism. Queen Cuboid and Princess Prism turned out to be fabulous rulers and never did anything daft like King Cube had.

The End

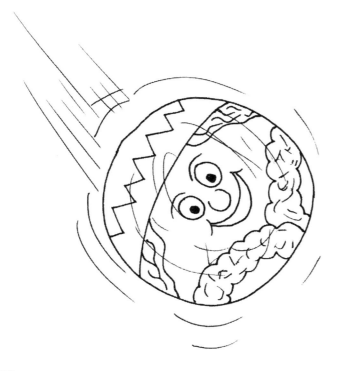

Programme of Study

KS1. Ma 2. 2c ... recognise that the position of a digit gives its value and know what each digit represents, including zero as a place holder...

Ma 2. 3b. ...find one half and one quarter of shapes and small numbers of objects...

Background

This story introduces the concept of place value in an imaginative context. The idea is that the first teacher in history, Miss /a/ has only nine pupils in her class. This is OK as numbers supposedly only go up to nine. However Miss /a/ becomes the first (but not the last) teacher to suffer the stress of teaching when more pupils arrive at her cave-classroom. To begin with she avoids the problem of dealing with numbers she can't record for the health and safety regulations (there are loads of regulations even in the stone age!) Being a brilliant teacher (like they all are so we've heard) she points out the fractions the class is divided up into on each occasion but when it rains and all the children end up in the cave-classroom a new solution is needed. Fortunately Medium /ae/ comes up with a solution – a new column!! The activities we suggest explore fractions and the idea of place value, for example but looking at alternatives to the place value system we use.

For fun we've given the characters names based on vowel phonemes using the Letters and Sounds system, knowing that the children will be exploring these phonemes at around this time in their learning development, so we hope it will be interesting for them to see them being used in a different context. You may find our publication "Every Phoneme Covered" a useful reference if you wish to expand or link phoneme teaching to this idea.

The names and their related phonemes are;

Miss /a/ (as in "cat")
Little /e/ and Big /e/ (as in "bed")
/i/ (as in "tin")
/o/ (as in "got")
/u/ (as in "up")
/ur/ (as in "work")
Loud /ae/, Medium /ae/ and Quiet /ae/ (as in "day")
/ee/ (as in "see")
/oo/ (as in "cook")
/ie/ (as in "pie")

Lesson plan

"About the importance of place value and how difficult it would be to use numbers without columns of different value."

"For you to investigate problems looking at the use of the different place value columns."

"Place value is an important feature of the numbers we use."

Activity One

A group of the children could imagine themselves to be at Stone Age School. One area is "inside" the cave, another "outside". Having arranged themselves in different combinations of ways, they can be asked to describe the similarities/differences between the two groups. First with words (e.g. "more", "fewer", "the same"). Then with numbers (e.g. 5 inside and 7 outside). It could be pointed out to the children that the total number of children is always the same however they arrange themselves – thus demonstrating conservation of number. The children could be asked to write down sums to match their particular groupings (e.g. 7 + 5 = 12, 7 − 5 = 2) or to find ways to demonstrate physically the sums given, e.g. in the last example 5 "inside" and "out" stand near to each other but the extra 2 stand apart from the rest to demonstrate the difference between the two groups.

Activity Two

This could develop from the above activity, except that the children are asked to describe the fraction of the total group, which is inside or outside the cave and/or arrange themselves to demonstrate given fractions.

Activity Three

The children could be asked to imagine that Miss /a/ and her class hadn't invented the ten's column – in fact that it still hasn't been invented. They could be asked to think about how we would be managing. Could we only have a maximum of 9 of everything, e.g. nine players in a football team, a speed limit of nine miles an hour, would we never be more than nine years old? How would we cope? Possibly the children could carry out this activity in the form of a drama exercise and then demonstrate to the rest of the class their ideas about how we could manage without a ten's column. A related idea might be to see if the children could invent new symbols for the numbers that we call 10, 11 etc but which are used in the units column. The children could discuss the pros and cons of the ideas they think of.

Activity Four

The children could be asked to think of other ways in which the ten's column might have been invented. To help the children focus on the fact that as we add more columns, we move the new digits to the left by imagining what numbers would look like if we added new columns to a number in different ways. What if we moved to the right? 170 would become 071. What if we added columns by going upwards?

0
7
1

Or diagonally?

1   0
    7   7
        0   1

Or wrote one column on top of another?

Activity Five

The children could demonstrate the systems they think of and demonstrate them to the rest of the class. There could then be a class discussion regarding the pros and cons of this method over the system that we now use. (It might be pertinent to point out that we have not always used the number system as we used it now. The Babylonians and Sumerians counted in 60s and despite using a place value of sorts, some ancient cultures didn't think of inventing a symbol like 0 to represent zero, or no number being in a particular column, which could often lead to confusion. (1007 might look the same as 107 when written as, 1   7 and 1 7!) Inventing zero was a major mathematical breakthrough!

It was probably first invented by the Mayans in South America before being invented in Europe about 200 years after the end of the Babylonian empire, during the time of Alexander the Great (and even then wasn't fully used until the 16th Century!). It was then later also invented by the Chinese.

Wednesday morning again

"Ah well," thought Miss /a/, the teacher of the first school in history. "It'll soon be the weekend."

Of course they didn't have a school bell in the stone age – or even the faintest dream what a bell was – so Miss /a/ banged a piece of flint against a rock to let the children know that the day had begun.

Of course as this was years before misbehaviour was discovered, all the children obediently filed into the cave, which acted as their schoolroom and went to sit behind their rocks. Miss /a/ walked to the front, sat behind her rock and began doing the register. This was the hardest work of the day because she had to carve the ticks or crosses onto a slab of rock with all the children's names already carved on it. All the children were present today and as she called out their names they grunted politely. There were the two /e/ brothers, Little /e/ and Big /e/, /i/, /o/, /u/,

/ur/ and the /ae/s, Loud /ae/, Medium /ae/ and Quiet /ae/. Nine children in all.

When she'd finally finished carving out the register and all the /ae/s (the oldest children) had helped her heave it out of the way, Miss /a/ was ready to start the day.

But just then there was a polite growl at the door of the cave-classroom. Everyone turned to look and saw a young girl standing at the mouth of the cave. "Hello," she grunted. "My name is /ee/. My family have just moved into the cave three holes away. Please can I come to your school?"

All the children were excited. It was always great to have more children in their pack for playing games like "Hunt the Tiger" of "Stun the Alligator".

But to the children's surprise, Miss /a/ reacted very strangely. "NOOOO!!!" she shrieked at the top of her voice. She was the first teacher in the world to experience the stress of

teaching (but not the last). "Look, we'd love you to join our school but we've already got as many children as we can have in it." she grunted politely.

"What do you mean, Miss?" grunted several of the children. "There's plenty of room in the cave-classroom."

"Oh, I know that," grunted Miss /a/. "That's not the problem."

"What is the problem then Miss?" grunted /i/.

"Well," explained Miss /a/. "So far there are nine of you in school. But that's as far as numbers go up to as you know. If /ee/ joins the school I won't know how many of you are in the school because numbers don't go up that far."

Everyone could understand the problem even though it felt very odd not being able to let /ee/ into the cave-classroom just because

they didn't have a number for explaining how many children there would be in the school if she joined them.

"Perhaps someone will invent some more numbers one day," grunted Loud /ae/ hopefully.

"But what do we do until then?" asked Miss /a/. "I have to know how many of you are in the classroom for the Health and Safety regulations," (There were loads of rules even in the Stone Age.)

Then /o/ had an idea. "Why don't I go and work outside with /ee/?" he grunted. "Then you could know the number of children inside the cave-classroom and the number outside it."

"That's a brilliant idea." grunted Miss /a/ excitedly. "It's a nice sunny day, so why don't all you /ae/s go outside with /o/ as well, and then all the oldest children will be outside and all the youngest inside!"

So that's exactly what happened. It was the Art lesson at school on a Wednesday. Miss /a/ got the youngest children to paint pictures of their favourite animals on the walls of the cave-classroom and got the older children to paint pictures of each other on the outside of the cave-classroom. Being a brilliant teacher, Miss /a/ pointed out to the children that with five children working inside and five working outside that the class had been split into two halves. It was the first lesson ever about fractions.

The day ended successfully and all the children had done lots of excellent paintings. "It looks like we'll be alright Miss, until someone invents some more numbers," grunted /ur/.

"I hope someone comes up with something quickly," grunted Miss /a/. "What if more families move into the local caves and even more children want to start at the school, what will we do then?"

"Dunno Miss," replied /ur/. It was the first time in History anyone ever said, "Dunno Miss," (but not the last).

They got the chance to find out the very next day because two new pupils, /oo/ and /ie/, turned up. To begin with Miss /a/ got very worked up again. She thought about taking sick leave but realised she couldn't because she was the only teacher in the whole world. But /o/ saved the day again by suggesting that as long as at least three of the children worked outside she would still be able to have a number for the children inside the cave-classroom and for the children outside. Miss /a/ agreed even though she was getting less and less happy about the situation.

So /o/, /ee/ and /ie/ worked outside while the rest of the children worked inside. It was the Design and Technology lesson at school on a Thursday. The children working inside the classroom were asked to see if they could work out better designs for carving arrowheads out of flint. The children working outside had to try carving models of each other out of different materials to see which worked the best. /o/ used chalk, /ee/ used clay and /ie/ used mud. Being a brilliant teacher (as I've said) Miss /a/ pointed out to the children that with three children outside and nine inside that meant the class had been split into quarters. One quarter of the children were outside and three-quarters were inside. It was the second lesson ever about fractions.

The day ended successfully and everyone had done lots of excellent work. "It really does look like we'll be alright until someone invents some more numbers, Miss," grunted /ur/ again.

"I still hope someone comes up with something quickly. What if another eight children join the school, what will we do then?" grunted Miss /a/ worrying about the worst possible thing which could happen.

"I don't think that's very likely," grunted /ur/ reassuringly.

Sure enough the next day eight new children didn't join the school, so Miss /a/ could relax for a little bit longer. It was Inventions Day at school on a Friday – everyone's favourite day.

Little /e/ asked three other children to work with her inside the cave on an invention she was working on to try and make things move around more easily. With her friends she was carving a boulder into a round shape.

"It's going to be called a wheel," she told everyone.

/o/ asked the rest of the children to work outside with him to help him try and make something which he saw in the forest in the summer when it had been really hot and dry. He thought it might be really good for keeping the caves warmer in the winter.

"I don't know what to call it yet," he told everyone. "I might call it "OUCH!!" because that's what I called it when I touched some of it!"

Being a brilliant teacher (as I may have mentioned before), Miss /a/ pointed out to the children that with four children inside the cave-classroom and eight children outside that meant the class had been split into thirds. One third of the children were inside and two-thirds were outside. It was the third lesson ever about fractions!

/o/ didn't have the faintest idea how to make "OUCH!!" He only knew what it looked like – and what it felt like! So he and his friends tried all sorts of ways of making it. To begin with they made a pile of leaves and twigs because /o/ remembered that they seemed to like "OUCH!!" the most. Then they tried running around the pile of twigs and leaves, grunting "OUCH!!" at them. That didn't work. Then they tried throwing things at the pile of leaves and twigs, like other twigs and also stones. That didn't work. They tried sitting on the pile of twigs and leaves to warm them up. That didn't work. But then they tried rubbing the sticks together to warm them up that way. /o/ got very excited when he saw something coming out of the twigs because he'd seen a lot of it when "OUCH!!" was around. Actually it was smoke but of course there wasn't a name for it then.

"I think we're onto something here, Miss!" grunted /o/, showing Miss /a/. But just then disaster struck! It suddenly began pouring with rain! The "OUCH!!" disappeared immediately! So did the children – into the cave-classroom!

Miss /a/ ran in frantically behind them. "AAAAAAAAGHHHHH!" she screamed. "What are we going to do now? There isn't a number to explain how many of you are in the cave-classroom!"

"Don't worry Miss, I've got an idea," grunted Medium /ae/.

"Go on," grunted Miss /a/.

"Well, it's like this Miss," she began. "The shape of Little /e/'s invention has given me an idea. I think we could draw a shape like that to show that nothing is there."

"Hmm," hmmed Miss /a/, not quite understanding the idea yet but not admitting that because (of course) she was a teacher. "Go on. What do you want to call this shape which shows that nothing is there?" she asked.

"I think I'll call it... "nought"," replied Medium /ae/, continuing. "So when there are no numbers at all, like when there's no one at school if we're ill or we're chasing a tiger out of the caves again, you could write a nought in the register – 0.

The smallest numbers would still be 1, 2, 3, 4, 5, 6, 7, 8, 9 but when the numbers can't get any bigger – like they couldn't when /ee/ then /oo/ and /ie/ came to school – why don't we do something new? Why don't we start the numbers off again in a new place, next to the column the smallest numbers were in? The new column could start with a one and the first column could start with a nought – 1 then 0. The nought would show that there isn't a number in the first column yet. Let's call that number ...um... "ten." That would have been the number of children in the school when /ee/ arrived on Wednesday.

Then the numbers after "ten" would be, 1 then 1, 1 then 2, 1 then 3, 1 then 4, 1 then 5, 1 then 6, 1 then 7, 1 then 8 and 1 then 9, as the numbers get bigger. That would mean that the number we would write for the number of children in the school when /oo/ and /ie/ arrived would be 1 then 2. I think I'll call this new number "toaster"... no... that doesn't sound right... "twelve"... yes that sounds better, I'll call it twelve.

We could call the first column with numbers in the units column and my new column the ten's column!"

"THAT'S BRILLIANT!!!" shouted Miss /a/, leaping up with excitement. "YOU'VE JUST INVENTED PLACE VALUE!!!!!....."

"How did you know that, Miss?" asked Medium /ae/.

"Um... I just did – I am a teacher you know," replied (and lied) Miss /a/. She just made it up as she went along – like most teachers. (Though it was much easier to do that in Miss /a/'s day).

Still the name for Medium /ae/'s invention, "place value" stuck, as did the name "nought" which Medium /ae/ had made up. In fact while it continued to pour outside the cave-classroom, the children and Miss /a/ made up the names for all the numbers which there could be because of them inventing a nought and a new column of numbers called the tens column.

By the time they had made up the name for and got to "ninety nine" the rain had stopped and it was time to go home.

"What are we going to do now we've used up both these columns?" asked /i/.

"Why don't we work that out next week?" suggested Miss /a/, who had a headache by now after making all these incredible breakthroughs in the number system and she just wanted to go and lie down for a while.

As Miss /a/ and the children came out of the cave-classroom, they were very upset to see that the paintings on the outside of the cave had been completely washed away. Also the models which had been made were now only sad lumps of chalk, clay and mud. (Luckily of course the paintings inside the cave-classroom and the flint arrowheads survived for us to discover thousands of years later). Also the twigs and leaves which /o/ and his friends had been using to try and invent "OUCH!!" were completely soaked.

"I think I'll call my invention "fire" not "OUCH!!" when I've invented it." grunted /o/.

"I shouldn't if I were you," replied Miss /a/. "That name will never stick."

And of course teachers are always right, aren't they?

The End

Programme of Study

KS1. Ma 2. 3b. ...understand multiplication as repeated addition...

Lesson plan

"That multiplication of numbers is actually repetition of addition."

"For you to work out a way of dancing a multiplication sequence ("table".)"

"The times tables of repeated addition are really useful to learn "off by heart" and dancing the tables may help you do this!"

The text explains the usefulness of learning multiplication sums as otherwise it's sometimes necessary to do very long sums (as anyone who hasn't learned the "times tables" can tell you!) In the story Julius Caesar gets annoyed with his senators having to add up ever longer repeated sequences of three The senators invent the times tables and realise they are useful to learn. As a way of making this fun we suggest a "times table dance". This uses physical signs/moments for each number, 1- 9, "times", "equals" and "-ty" (as in Twen-ty – demonstrated by doing the sign for 2 followed by "ty".) There are suggested movements illustrated here but maybe you and the children could work out movements of your own. Having worked out how to do one particular times table, e.g. the x2 table you could differentiate this activity by getting the children to work out how to "dance" other times tables, which may be an opportunity for them to work out what the sums would be at the same time as working out the necessary movements!

"If you think some of the children, maybe some of the boys for example, wouldn't like the idea of a "dance" you could describe the activity as a "times table workout"!"

Times table dance

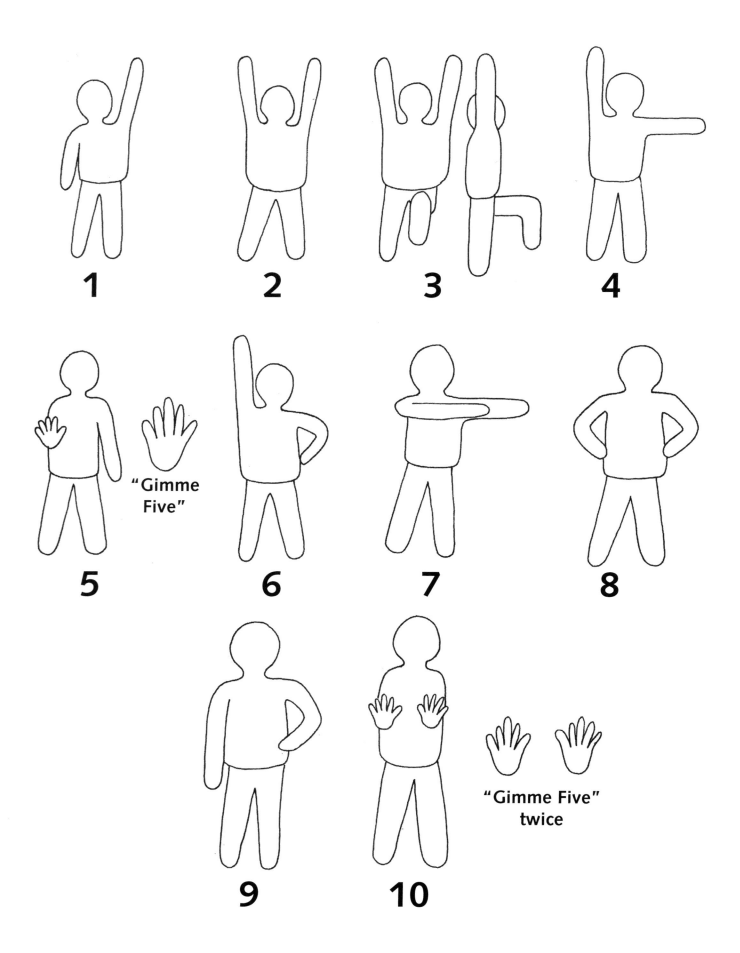

1

2

3

4

5 "Gimme Five"

6

7

8

9

10 "Gimme Five" twice

Using stories to teach **Maths** *Ages 4-7*

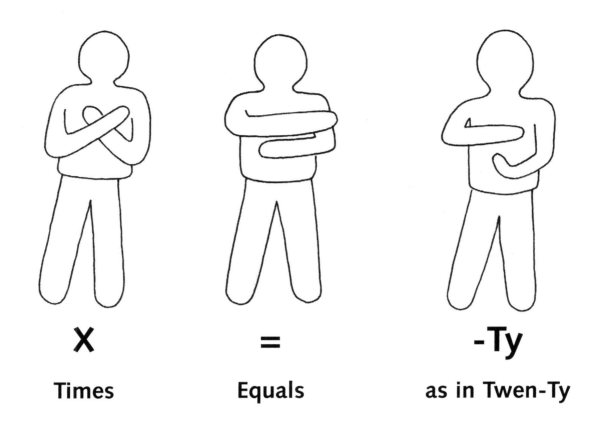

X

Times

=

Equals

-Ty

as in Twen-Ty

3 **X** **4** **=** **1** **2**

Chariot Champions

It was another sunny day in Ancient Rome. Great Caesar, the Roman Emperor, had decided to have a day off from conquering barbarians and decided to relax by going to the amphitheatre to watch some chariot races. There hadn't been chariot races on the programme at the amphitheatre that day but as soon as Caesar announced that he wanted to see chariot races, suddenly there were. Caesar enjoyed being ruler of the known world because he nearly always did exactly what he wanted to do on his days off. The slaves had to feed the lions normal meat rather than the nice juicy prisoners that they had been going to have when throwing prisoners to the lions had still been on the programme.

Caesar had a special throne high up in the amphitheatre. It was hard work just climbing up to it. Not that that bothered Caesar because he was carried on a chair carried by eight slaves. Caesar didn't care about the slaves. It was their fault for being slaves by allowing him to capture them when he conquered the land they'd lived in as far as he was concerned.

When he had sat down on his special throne and the crowd had stopped cheering him, he decided he wanted to get the attention of one of his slaves called Anthony.

"Mark Anthony what Great Caesar has to say to you!" said Caesar.

"I'm marking oh Great Caesar," replied Anthony. He knew he didn't have much choice. If Anthony didn't mark Caesar, he knew he'd be on the menu for the lions when they next had a feast.

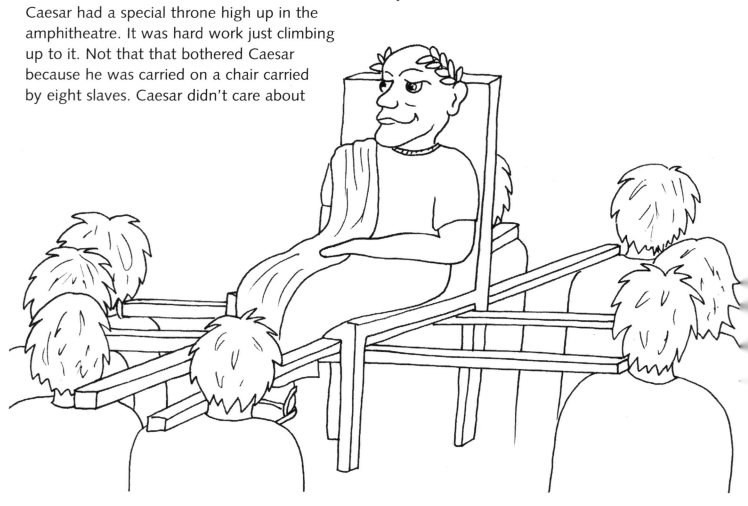

"As you know We sent a proclamation all over Rome this morning saying that We wanted to see as many brave young men as possible competing in the chariot race," continued Caesar. (Caesar always said "We" when he meant "I" because he was such a big head. Still rulers of the known world usually are.)

"Yes we di...I mean you did Oh Mighty Caesar," said Anthony.

"Caesar wishes to know how many brave young men there are in Rome. Go to the starting blocks and find out how many brave young men have entered the race."

"Yes Oh Wondrous Caesar. Whatever you ask is performed immediately," replied Anthony, knowing that was what he was supposed to say. He would much rather have said something like, "GO TO THE STARTING BLOCKS??? BUT I'VE JUST HELPED CARRY YOU UP HERE AND IT'S MILES TO THE STARTING BLOCKS!!! I'M EXHAUSTED!!!" but that just wasn't the thing you said to Caesar, unless you'd gone mad and desperately wanted to be lion meat.

So poor Anthony walked all the way to the starting blocks. When he got there he discovered that only two chariots were lined up behind them. Both contained the three brave men it took to drive a racing chariot.

"The Boss won't like this," thought Anthony as he trudged all the way back to Caesar.

He was right. When he finally returned, Caesar said; "Tell Us how many brave young men have entered the chariot race."

"There's three plus three men, Oh Great Caesar," replied Anthony. Being only a slave he wasn't supposed to be able to count to more than five and as you can tell Anthony knew when to keep his mouth shut about things.

"How many men is that?" Caesar asked his senators who were sitting around him. Caesar didn't know anything apart from how to conquer places and be big headed.

"Why three plus three makes six Oh Great Caesar," replied Brutus, one of the senators. It really upset Brutus to be ruled by a Caesar that was so useless at mathematics. One day he was going to teach him a lesson somehow.

"WHAT!!! ARE THERE BUT SIX BRAVE YOUNG MEN IN ROME!!??!!!" boomed Caesar going the same colour purple as his tunic. "What's this Empire coming to? I don't know – the youth of today!" (That by the way is the first recorded moment of someone saying, "I don't know – the youth of today!" As far as we know, people have been saying that ever since.) "I can't believe it! Go back to the starting blocks Anthony and see whether any more brave young men have entered the race."

"BUT!!!..." began Anthony angrily before he remembered to control himself. Luckily for him, Brutus sneezed at the same time.

"ACHOO!!"

"Bless you, Brutae," said Caesar.

"Thank you, Great Caesar," said Brutus. It really annoyed him that Caesar never got his name right either. "I seem to have a cold coming on."

"And flu Brutae?" asked Caesar.

"No I don't think so," replied Brutus, wishing he could say, "WILL YOU GET MY NAME RIGHT JUST ONCE YOU STUPID MAN!!!…" but realising that senators taste the same to lions as slaves, he kept his mouth shut for the moment.

"One day you'll call me Brutae once too often," thought Brutus to himself.

Meanwhile poor exhausted Anthony was trudging back to the starting blocks. "If I wasn't a slave I'd give up my job," he thought to himself. When he got back to the starting blocks he found that another two chariots had been entered into the race.

"I still don't think the Boss'll be too pleased," thought Anthony as he began the long journey back to Caesar's throne.

He was right. When he finally returned, Caesar again said; "Tell Us how many brave young men have entered the chariot race."

"There's three plus three plus three plus three men, oh Mighty Caesar," replied Anthony.

"By all the Gods! How many men is that??" Caesar asked his senators.

"Er, I think that makes ten," said Casca.

"No isn't it thirteen?" asked Cinna.

"But I thought it made eleven," said Cassius.

None of the senators had heard Anthony's message properly so they made him repeat his message slowly so they could work it out – which made Caesar even more impatient. When he was finally told it came to twelve he blew a fuse – if he'd known what a fuse was back then.

"WHAT??? ARE THERE BUT TWELVE BRAVE YOUNG MEN IN ROME!!??!" boomed Caesar

making the purple in his tunic look pale. "What's the point of me going abroad and conquering more land if I come home to be surrounded by a bunch of wimps!!??!!"

The senators all looked at each other. They lived in Rome too and wondered whether Caesar was talking about them as well. They weren't pleased.

"I can't believe it! Go back to the starting blocks Anthony and see whether any more brave men have entered the race." Caesar commanded.

"WHAT?" began Anthony angrily before he remembered to control himself again. Luckily for him Brutus burped at the same time.

"Burp!"

"You seem to have indigestion Brutae," said Caesar.

"Yes, I ate two chickens for my tea, Mighty Caesar."

"Ate two Brutae? Then you fooled Caesar. I thought you only ate one."

"No Great Caesar," replied Brutus. It really annoyed him that Caesar could always stuff himself with two whole chickens and never get indigestion.

Meanwhile poor very exhausted Anthony was trudging back to the starting blocks. "I should get double pay for this," he thought to himself. But then as he didn't get any pay, he realised that wouldn't make any difference.

When he got back to the starting blocks, he found that another four chariots had been entered into the race.

"I still don't think the Boss'll be too pleased," thought Anthony as he began the long journey back to Caesar's throne. He was right. When he finally returned, Caesar again said; "Tell Us how many brave young men have entered the chariot race?"

"There's three plus three plus three plus three plus three plus three plus three plus three men, oh Mighty Caesar," replied Anthony.

"By all the Gods… and any others we haven't made up yet – how many men is that?" Caesar asked his senators.

"Er…" said most of the senators.

"Um…" said the rest of the senators. None of them had been able to follow Anthony's message properly so they had to make him repeat it slowly again. Even then they couldn't agree so they had to make him repeat it a second time – which as you might have guessed didn't make Caesar happy at all. When he was finally told that it came to twenty-four men he nearly decided to throw the entire audience to the lions!

"WHAT!!! ARE THERE BUT TWENTY-FOUR BRAVE YOUNG MEN IN ROME!!??!!" boomed Caesar going a completely new shade of purple that has never been seen before or since. "Right you senators, you go and see whether any more brave young men have entered the race… and if they haven't you lot enter instead… and for goodness sake don't come back with another enormous message!"

All of the senators opened their mouths because they all nearly told Caesar to get stuffed but they all just managed to control themselves. Being senators they were very big headed, just like Caesar and they didn't like being ordered about but they realised that if they said anything at the moment they soon wouldn't have a head – however big it was. All the senators began to move off, except Brutus who didn't think Caesar meant him as well.

"You too Brutae. Don't fool with Caesar," said Caesar, making it very clear that Brutus was included.

"Yes, oh Great Caesar," replied Brutus, only just managing not to sound very very annoyed.

The only person who was at all happy was Anthony. He went and squatted down with the other slaves and had a well-earned rest. "One day there'll be a law against this," said Anthony.

"A law against slavery, not for a very very long time," replied Lucius, one of the other slaves. He was right.

Meanwhile the senators were grumbling to each other as they trudged to the starting blocks.

"That Caesar is getting far too big for his sandals," said Cinna

"And too tall for his toga," agreed Cassius.

"And too large for his laurels," agreed Casca.

"We'll have to do something about it someday," said Brutus.

By this time they had reached the starting blocks. To their relief they found that another two chariots had entered the race. None of them had looked forward to the prospect of racing themselves.

"What are we going to tell Caesar when we get back though?" asked Cassius. "We can't say, "There are three plus three plus three plus three plus three plus three plus three plus three plus three plus three men competing, or he'll do his nut!"

"There must be some better way of working out groups of numbers rather than having to add them up all the time," said Cinna.

"Eureka!" shouted Brutus. It was a word the Romans had stolen from the Greeks (just like nearly everything else). It means, "I've got it!" Brutus had hit upon the idea of multiplication as a way of adding up sequences of the same number much more quickly.

The senators worked out all the numbers in the three times multiplication table.

"Now all we've got to do is work out all the other multiplication tables for the other numbers and adding up sequences of the same number will be much faster!!" said Brutus excitedly.

Although Caesar was fairly pleased to hear that thirty brave young men had entered the chariot race, he wasn't very excited about Brutus's invention called multiplication.

"All we will have to do is learn our multiplication tables and we will all be able to add up much more quickly, oh Great Caesar!" said Brutus.

"I can't be bothered," said Caesar.

One day Brutus and his fellow senators punished Caesar far harder for not being bothered to learn his multiplication tables than your teacher ever will.

The End

The king-sized take away pizza for the Queen

Programme of Study

KS1. Ma 2 1a. approach problems involving number, and data presented in a variety of forms, in order to identify what they need to do.

Ma 2 3a. understand subtraction as both "take away" and "difference" and use the related vocabulary… … solve simple missing number problems.

Lesson plan

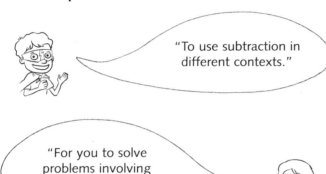

"To use subtraction in different contexts."

"For you to solve problems involving subtraction."

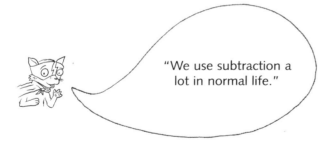

"We use subtraction a lot in normal life."

In this case the story itself is both story and resource as the children have to solve this subtraction challenges within the story as Pietro the chef is ordered to remove some of the unusual toppings he has added to a pizza ordered for the Queen by her head butler. The accompanying poem explores one possible technique for working out subtraction challenges and could be a springboard for a class discussion about different ways of carrying out subtraction e.g. knowing particular results off by heart, counting on, counting back (as in the poem) etc. As we all think in different ways our experience is that it is useful to show children different strategies for solving problems so that they can hone in on strategies that work for them most of the time but are aware of other strategies that may work in different contexts.

As a follow up session we have the following suggestions;

- The class group could be split into halves to play "Subtraction challenge". Each team have to work out subtraction challenges (checked by you for the questioners knowing the right answer and for appropriateness, i.e. suitable challenging but not ridiculous!) and ask the opposing team for the solution. A correct answer wins a point. An incorrect answer is a point for the other team.

- Ask the children to write stories similar to "The king-sized take away pizza for the Queen" including subtraction challenges to try out on the other children when they are presented to the class.

- Cover the figures used in the story with a small bit of sticky note paper and photocopy the story. The children then can make up new figures of the numbers of toppings and can try out the challenges on the other children in the class or on children from other classes that they read the stories too.

The king-sized take away pizza for the Queen

Well, it's like this y'see. I run "Pietro's Take Away Pizzas" in Victoria Street, which just 'appens to be the nearest take away pizza joint near Her Majesty's main bedsit – Buckin'am Palace.

This particular evenin' as the Royal Cooks was cookin' the Royal Dinner (and the dinner for all her guests, family and staff) the Royal Electric Cookers all broke down with a Royal Fizz and all the Royal Gas Ovens broke down with a Royal Pop.

Result – No way the Royal Cooks could cook the Royal Din-Dins. This was a right Royal Problem because the Queen 'ad invited the

President of Turkey to tea. Fortunately her advisors told 'Er that the President liked Pizza. So that's when I gets a Royal Phone Call on the Royal Dog and Bone.

A take away pizza order from the Queen! Well, not exactly the Queen! It was a bloke called The Royal Under Butler or somefing. I doubt they 'ad a Royal Take Away Pizza Orderer 'cos 'e'd 'ave been unemployed up until then.

Anyway, he told me 'e'd be over in 'arf an 'our to pick it up and check if it was OK for Her Nibbs. I was pleased about that 'as I dint fink I'd be able to deliver a special King-Sized pizza to the Queen on the back ov one ov our scooters.

This must be the first Royal Take Away Pizza order in 'Istory I fort, so I'm going to make the MOST AMAZING pizza that 'as ever been seen!

The base was the size of a paddling pool. Actually don't tell HRH but I did actually mix it up in me kids paddling pool. We 'ad to cut the dough in slices and cook them separately then put 'em all back together again in a circle.

Then, using every saucepan in the place and three months supply of tomato puree, I 'eated up the puree and then poured it over the base.

Meanwhile all me staff were busily grating every bit of cheese we could find in our three fridges. We must 'ave used every type of cheese you could imagine. We even used some Walrus Cheese we found at the back of the fridge, which must 'ave been given to us sometime as a sample. All the grated cheese then went on the pizza.

That brought me to the part of makin' pizza I most enjoy – addin' the toppin'. I used ABSOLUTELY everythin' I 'ad available in the place! Onions, mushrooms, peppers, salami, pineapple, peas, carrots, baked beans, bacon, cornflakes… the lot! I'd never 'ad so much fun! I was just finishin' it off when the In Between Butler, or whatever 'e was, turned up. Sure enough 'e'd come in a horse-drawn carriage. Lucky it was an open-top carriage, I fort, otherwise we'd 'ave never got it through the door.

"'Ere you are!" I declared, indicating the pizza. Not that you could miss it, it filled up nearly half the shop and some parts of it that didn't fit on the table were propped up with stools.

I'd never been so proud ov anyfing I'd done in all my life but as soon as the Inside Out Butler looked at it, I knew there was a problem.

"Some of these toppings will have to be removed," he said.

"You mean take 'em away?" I asked.

"Exactly," he replied.

"What?" I asked. "All ov them?"

"No, only some."

"Such as?"

"Well one just knows that Prince Philip won't like those Fried Fillets of Fresh French Fish. Take six of them away."

Well I'd put 10 on the pizza, so that left ____.

"Anyfing else?" I asked.

"The President of Turkey doesn't like chicken. Take 4 of those roast chickens away."

Well, I'd only put 9 roast chickens on it, so when I'd taken away 4, that left ____.

"None of the princesses will be able to eat the dried peas. For some reason they can't sleep if they eat too many. Remove about 50 of them."

There must 'ave been about 100 dried peas on the pizza, so when I'd taken away 50 that left ____. Lucky I still left them in the boxes I thought to me self.

Then the Sideways Up Butler tells me that Edward was bored of eating ice cream and told me to remove 6 of the scoops of Cabbage flavoured ice cream I'd put on the pizza. There

were only 13 scoops of Cabbage flavoured ice cream to start with, so that left _____.

"Prince Charles doesn't like King Prawns for some reason, remove 12 of them," was my next order. I'd only used 20, so once I'd taken away 12 that left _____.

Apparently the Middle Butler knew that Andrew drew the line at having too many chocolate éclairs on a pizza. (I 'ave to admit I thought to me self, 'ow on earth does 'e know that when Andrews' probably never 'ad a pizza but still). So I 'ad to remove 7 out of 14 of the chocolate éclairs, leavin' me wiv _____.

Then he explains that William ate enough haggis at college, so he doesn't want any on his pizza, so I removed 5 out of the 12 haggises, leaving only _____.

"It seems 'Arry 'ad enough 'addock in the Army, so I 'ad to take away 8 of the 14 'addock, leaving only ___.

Kate Middleton is avoidin' cakes to keep loverly and slim, so I 'ad to take 6 of the 18 cup cakes off the pizza, leaving only ___.."

After that he told me that the Head Butler didn't like turkey legs, so I 'ad to remove 9 out of the 15 I'd put on, leaving me with _____.

He fort the guards would be guarded about 'avin' too many prunes on their bit of pizza, especially as they 'ad to stand still for so long, so I 'ad to remove 25 out ov 40, leavin' only _____.

Thinkin' about it, we both agreed that the corgis would probably fight over the bananas, especially if two of them grabbed opposite ends at the same time. I took off 13 of the 18 bananas I'd put on, leaving _____.

Finally the Somewhere Butler revealed the biggest surprise. Apparently the Beefeaters don't eat beef! So I removed 22 of the 34 slices of beef I'd used, leaving only _____.

At last the Upside Down Butler was satisfied and 'e and the pizza were carried off in the carriage.

A few days later, I got a card from the Queen. It said, "One really enjoyed one's pizza. So did everyone else. Next time though One wondered if you could leave off the crisps and the yoghurt."

As you can imagine, I was totally chuffed! After that success I sent a menu to No 10 Downing Street. I 'aven't 'ad a call yet but maybe 'is ovens 'aven't broken down yet. Who knows?

The End

I'm counting on you counting back to subtract!

We hope we will give satisfaction,
With our method of subtraction

Our method gets you to count back
So "take away's" will be on track!

Choose a number good and high,
And to that number say "goodbye."

Count back down the number line,
Then my friend you're doing fine.

If you buy things from a shop,
Your counting back may never stop!

Start with ten and count back three,
Then down to seven is where you'll be.

Then pay for something with pounds five,
And down at two you will arrive.

Two take two leaves you with none…
SO YOU CAN'T DO ANY MORE SHOPPING!!

Programme of Study

KS1. Ma 2 1a. approach problems involving number, and data presented in a variety of forms, in order to identify what they need to do.

Ma 2 3a. understand addition and use related vocabulary... understand subtraction as both "take away" and "difference" and use related vocabulary... solve simple missing number problems.

Ma 2 3b. understand multiplication as repeated addition... ... find one half of... small numbers... use vocabulary associated with multiplication...

Lesson plan

"How to solve a challenge using number skills."

"To solve a challenge using your skills with numbers!"

The challenges here involve solving problems of more than one step, mainly involving addition and subtraction but also some multiplication/doubling and division/halving. To complete the first challenge the children need to be able to see the illustration of the pirates waiting in "The Numberline" with their treasure maps, waiting for "pirates" like Jim with the second half of the treasure map and the information sheet so that they can work out who is the correct pirate for Jim to team up with.

Resources

The pirates in "The Numberline" illustration.

Information about the pirates.

Resource worksheets.

The pirates in "The Numberline"

Using stories to teach **Maths** *Ages 4-7*

Longbeard has the map for Easter Island.

Falsebeard has the map for Bank Holiday Island.

Blondbeard has the map for Half-term Island.

Shortbeard has the maps for Christmas Island.

Hairybeard has the maps for Next Week Island.

Gingerbeard has the map for Last Wednesday Island.

Worksheet 1: Finding the right pirate

Name: _____

The right pirate had 5 parrots, 3 flew away and he bought 1.

Number of parrots _____

The right pirate had 6 swords, broke 5 and was given 3.

Number of swords _____

The right pirate had 7 ear-rings, lost 3, then found 4.

Number of ear-rings _____

Who was the right pirate?

_____

Which is the right island?

_____

Name: _____

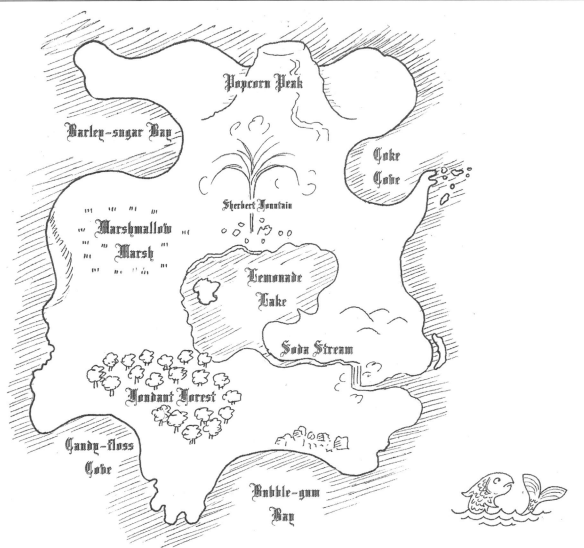

To find the treasure start at Sherbet Fountain. Head towards Marshmallow Marsh. Take 5 paces forwards, then back 3 then 1 forwards. Number of paces _____

Now turn towards the Fondant Forest. Take 6 paces forwards, then 4 paces back and then 7 forwards. Number of paces _____

Now head towards Bubble-gum Bay. Take 3 paces forwards, twice that many forwards again, then 2 back. Number of paces _____

Finally head towards Soda Stream. Take 8 paces forwards, then 4 back, then twice 4 paces forwards. Number of paces _____

Well done shipmates, you're now ready to dig for treasure!!!

Worksheet 3: Opening the treasure chest

Name: _____

The first number on the lock is 6, take 4, then add 2. First number _____

The second number is 12, take 5, then take 3 more. Second number _____

The third number is twice 5, then take 4. Third number _____

The fourth number is half of 8, then add 5. Fourth number _____

The fifth number is half of 10, then take 3 and add 7. Fifth number _____

Final code

_____

Well done shipmates!!!

Hello everyone. My name is Jim Crow. I've come to tell you my story because I need your help. Let me tell you how it all started.

I was having my breakfast one morning, when my Mum told me that she was a pirate. I was amazed.

"But I thought you were a dentist," I said.

"Oh, I'm one of those too," she said. "But when I'm not being a dentist I'm a pirate. I'm known on the Seven Seas as Nobeard. Like all my friends I'm a modern pirate of course. We just hunt for treasure, we don't hurt anyone."

"Do you say "Ho Ho Ho" at all?" I asked.

"Oh all the time and "Yo Ho Ho" and "Way Hay Me Hearties." Anyway the reason I've told you I'm a pirate is because I'm retiring from piracy. I want to spend more time helping people look after their teeth. The thing is I've still got half a treasure map to find some treasure. So as you've got nothing to do today I want you to go and find it."

"But I'm not a pirate," I said.

"You're the son of a pirate, that's nearly the same thing," said Mum.

"I'm not sure I want to hunt for treasure," I said.

"Well you've got a choice. You can either hunt for the treasure or clean your football boots." said Mum.

"O.K." I said. "What do I have to do?"

"Well, the first thing you've got to do is find the other pirate with the other half of the map. That map tells you which island to sail to and when the two halves are put together you'll both have clues about how to find where the treasure chest is buried on the island and clues about how to open the lock on the treasure chest when you've dug it up." said Mum.

"Where will I find this pirate?" I asked.

"You'll find the other pirate in a pub called "The Numberline". Mind you, you could have a problem when you get there because it's full of other pirates who are waiting for pirates with the other half of their treasure maps." said Mum.

"How do I know which pirate I'm looking for then?" I asked.

"I don't know..." said Mum.

"That's useful," I said interrupting. "I might as well go and clean my football boots then."

"I don't know but there are clues on your map," said Mum finishing her sentence and giving me one of her telling-me-off-without-saying-anything looks. I wondered if she'd learned it from being a pirate.

Well I looked at all the clues on my half of the map and sure enough there were also two clues to find the right pirate. I could tell that I wouldn't be able to work out any of the clues without loads of help. So please will you help me? I've given the map to your teacher. She's a friend of my Mum's. I don't think she's a pirate though. I'm not sure...

To read when challenges completed

Hello, it's Jim again! I just wanted to say thanks for your help! With your help I found the right pirate. We found where the treasure was buried and we were able to unlock the treasure chest! Inside it was full of a wonderful treasure! Loads and loads of exciting books about mathematics... oh and loads of gold, silver and jewels as well.

The End

Exciting times at the "Painthorpe Times"

Programme of Study

KS1. Ma 2 1a. approach problems involving number, and data presented in a variety of forms, in order to identify what they need to do.

Ma 2 3b. understand multiplication as repeated addition; understand that halving is the inverse of doubling and find one half and one quarter of shapes and small numbers of objects… … use vocabulary associated with multiplication…

. . . .

Lesson plan

"To understand multiplication sums written in everyday language."

"To find solutions to multiplication sums that are written in everyday language."

"We sometimes need to use multiplication skills in everyday situations."

The challenges here all involve multiplication, so the story links with "Chariot champions", which explores multiplication as repeated addition, so this story could also/alternatively be used as a way of introducing the "times table dance" idea that we've linked with that story. However the story itself here provides the lesson/challenge. The children could work out the problems with you as a class or in groups supported by you and T.A's. As further work the children could be asked to write their own alternative story, or you could cover the figures in the story with sticky note paper and photocopy the story, so that the children can replace the figures with figures that they work out and then present to other children in the class.

Exciting times at the "Painthorpe Times"

Hi, my name is Andrew Miles. I'm a newspaper editor. I've edited several successful newspapers but one of my most interesting jobs was editing an unsuccessful newspaper. It was called the "Painthorpe Times", a generally sensible name since it was published in the small town of Painthorpe. However when I was taken on to try and help the paper, it looked like the only news in the area was how badly the paper was doing!

I could soon see why the paper was dying on its feet. The few reporters still working for the paper thought that nothing interesting was going on in Painthorpe and were trying to put a local slant on national news.

"People don't want to read national and international news in a local paper!" I told my reporters. "People want to read what they most love reading about – themselves! Now to get this paper back on its legs again, we're not just going to mention a few people. We're going to try and find a way of mentioning as many people's names as possible! Whatever's going on, no matter how non-newsworthy you think it is, we're going to get creative and report it and mention everybody's name! Every name we mention is another paper sold!!

So that week we reported about…

The two pantomime donkeys in the local show. With two people in each donkey that sold two lots of two papers, making _____ papers.

The ten pairs of parents who entered the two-legged race at one of the school sports days. That sold two lots of ten papers, making _____ papers.

The nine Mc Mad people in each of the two local haggis tasting clubs. That sold _____ papers.

The eight choir members of the two local choirs and the competition they were in. That was another _____ papers sold.

The spectacular defeats suffered by the three local five-a-side teams. We made the players all sound a lot less terrible than they really were. So we sold _____ papers.

We reviewed the music of the six local bands that were in a "Battle of the Bands" competition. There were five people in each band, so we sold another _____ papers. We decided not to tell anyone that their music was only good for scaring cats.

It turned out that each week eight teams entered the quiz night competition at the local pub called, "The Proper Fraction". As there were four people in each team and we mentioned each person in our report about them; that sold _____ papers.

We found out that three people attended each service at the eight local churches on a Sunday, so we did a report about that. So we sold another _____ papers.

As this tactic began to work, we started to get really ambitious, silly almost but it worked!

We discovered that 40 people went to each of the three local nightclubs and they all wanted to see their name in the local paper. Because of that we sold _____ papers.

60 people went to one of the two local cinemas the night we asked them all for their names. So the next day we sold _____ papers.

200 people work at the four local factories. We squeezed in everyone's name, so we sold _____ papers!

150 children go to each of the five primary schools, making _____ children in all. (And that many families who want to buy the paper!!)

Well, having got the paper back on its feet again, I moved onto another paper. Maybe you could imagine who you'd sell the paper to if you were the editor of the "Painthorpe Times" instead of me. Remember, its not news that sells local papers but people's names.

The End

Hugh the ostrich detective and the town clown

Programme of Study

KS1. Ma 2 1a. approach problems involving number, and data presented in a variety of forms, in order to identify what they need to do.

Ma 2 3b. understand multiplication as repeated addition… … use vocabulary associated with multiplication…

· ·

Lesson plan

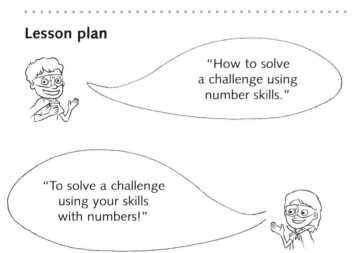

"How to solve a challenge using number skills."

"To solve a challenge using your skills with numbers!"

The investigations here – to find out who the best clown in town is (Blobbo as it happens) involve skills centred around multiplication but also use of the provided information, usually poshly called "data". The investigations come in pairs and could be carried out either by different groups of children, one pair after another, or altogether in sequence, as they help gradually eliminate the other clowns. The first two investigations list 30 clowns, from which many clowns can be eliminated – some are the same but many are different, so you could have a kind of suspect list that you/the children use to cross off clowns eliminated from the running. By the end of the first two investigations the list should be down to six candidates. The second two investigations eliminate three runners (Clowny in both cases) so the "suspect list" idea could still be used until finally Blobbo is identified! Good luck and may the force be with you… well with the children maths detectives I suppose…

· ·

Resources

Investigation resource sheets.

Resource sheet one.

Name: _____

Very Honest Sid tells Hugh the clue he knows about the best clown in town. It's that;

"… the best clown's trousers are four times twenty centimetres long and that his top hat is four times taller than his bowler hat, which is ten centimetres tall."

Can you use Very Honest Sid's clues to work out from this list Hugh has made of all the clowns in town to see which of them could be the best clown in town?

Nutty Trousers 60 cm Top hat 30 cm	Twitty Trousers 70 cm Top hat 50 cm	Nitty Trousers 70 cm Top hat 50 cm
Laugho Trousers 80 cm Top hat 40 cm	He He Trousers 70 cm Top hat 50 cm	Silly Trousers 80 cm Top hat 40 cm
Clowny Trousers 80 cm Top hat 40 cm	Dafto Trousers 70 cm Top hat 50 cm	Bloppy Trousers 80 cm Top hat 40 cm
Giggles Trousers 60 cm Top hat 30 cm	Witty Trousers 80 cm Top hat 40 cm	Gonzo Trousers 80 cm Top hat 40 cm
Blippy Trousers 80 cm Top hat 40 cm	Blobbo Trousers 80 cm Top hat 40 cm	Ho Ho Trousers 80 cm Top hat 50 cm
Ha Ha Trousers 70 cm Top hat 50 cm	Crumpet Trousers 60 cm Top hat 30 cm	Claude Trousers 70 cm Top hat 50 cm
Fiona Trousers 60 cm Top hat 30 cm	Clarence Trousers 70 cm Top hat 40 cm	Claire Trousers 80 cm Top hat 50 cm
Dill Trousers 70 cm Top hat 40 cm	Smiles Trousers 80 cm Top hat 40 cm	Jokey Trousers 80 cm Top hat 40 cm
Funny Trousers 70 cm Top hat 50 cm	Clumpy Trousers 60 cm Top hat 30 cm	Bonzo Trousers 60 cm Top hat 30 cm
Jumpy Trousers 80 cm Top hat 40 cm	Trippy Trousers 80 cm Top hat 40 cm	Tony Trousers 60 cm Top hat 30 cm

Investigation 2: Shoes and silly guns

Name: _____

Totally Truthful Ted tells Hugh the clue he knows about the best clown in town. It's that;

"… the best clown's silly shoes are five times longer than eight centimetres and his silly gun that shoots out a flag which says "BANG" is six times longer than four centimetres long."

Can you use Totally Truthful Ted's clues to work out from this list Hugh has made of all the clowns in town to see which of them could be the best clown in town?

Nutty Shoes 50 cm Gun 26 cm	Twitty Shoes 30 cm Gun 24 cm	Nitty Shoes 30 cm Gun 22 cm
Laugho Shoes 40 cm Gun 24 cm	He He Shoes 40 cm Gun 24 cm	Silly Shoes 40 cm Gun 24 cm
Clowny Shoes 40 cm Gun 24 cm	Dafto Shoes 50 cm Gun 26 cm	Bloppy Shoes 50 cm Gun 26 cm
Giggles Shoes 50 cm Gun 26 cm	Witty Shoes 30 cm Gun 22 cm	Gonzo Shoes 40 cm Gun 24 cm
Blippy Shoes 40 cm Gun 24 cm	Blobbo Shoes 40 cm Gun 24 cm	Ho Ho Shoes 50 cm Gun 26 cm
Ha Ha Shoes 30 cm Gun 22 cm	Crumpet Shoes 40 cm Gun 24 cm	Claude Shoes 40 cm Gun 26 cm
Fiona Shoes 40 cm Gun 24 cm	Clarence Shoes 30 cm Gun 22 cm	Claire Shoes 40 cm Gun 24 cm
Dill Shoes 40 cm Gun 26 cm	Smiles Shoes 30 cm Gun 24 cm	Jokey Shoes 30 cm Gun 22 cm
Funny Shoes 40 cm Gun 24 cm	Clumpy Shoes 30 cm Gun 22 cm	Bonzo Shoes 40 cm Gun 24 cm
Jumpy Shoes 30 cm Gun 22 cm	Trippy Shoes 50 cm Gun 26 cm	Tony Shoes 50 cm Gun 26 cm

Name: _____

Never Lies Larry tells Hugh the clues he knows about the best clown in town. It's that;

"… the best clown has got three times as many stars on his jacket than circles and twice as many suns than moons."

Can you use Never Lies Larry's clues to work out from photos Hugh has made of the remaining clowns on his list wearing their jackets to see which of them could be the best clown in town?

Gonzo's jacket is decorated with 5 stars, 2 circles, 6 suns and 3 moons.

Laugho's jacket is decorated with 3 stars, I circle, 5 suns and 4 moons.

Silly's jacket is decorated with 12 stars, 4 circles, 2 suns and 1 moon.

Blippy's jacket is decorated with 3 stars, I circle, 10 suns and 5 moons.

Clowny's jacket is decorated with 10 stars, 3 circles, 4 suns and 1 moon.

Blobbo's jacket is decorated with 9 stars, 3 circles, 6 suns and 3 moons.

Investigation 4: Custard and custard, banana skins and horns

Name: _____

Good Gail tells Hugh the clues she knows about the best clown in town. It's that;

"… the best clown has got four times as many custard pies to squash in peoples faces as jugs full of custard to pour down their trousers. Also he's got six times as many banana skins to slip on as horns which make silly noises."

Can you use Good Gail's clues to work out from photos Hugh has made of the remaining clowns on his list wearing their jackets to see which of them could be the best clown in town?

Gonzo has 4 custard pies, 1 jug of custard, 18 banana skins, 3 silly horns.

Laugho has 12 custard pies, 3 jugs of custard, 6 banana skins, I silly horn.

Silly has 6 custard pies, 1 jug of custard, 12 banana skins, 2 silly horns.

Blippy has 8 custard pies, 2 jugs of custard, 10 banana skins, 2 silly horns.

Clowny has 4 custard pies, 2 jugs of custard, 8 banana skins, 3 silly horns.

Blobbo has 4 custard pies, 1 jug of custard, 12 banana skins, 2 silly horns.

Hugh the ostrich detective and the town clown

Hello children, I'm Hugh the ostrich detective. You've probably heard of me. If you haven't you have now... I'm Hugh the ostrich detective... have we got that bit sorted out yet? Anyway I'm always out and about solving difficult crimes and mysteries. The story I'm going to tell you about though began when I was in between cases and was sitting in my office, twiddling my feathers, with nothing to do. I decided to go to the local police station to see if they had any cases for me because I was always solving cases for them.

"I'm afraid we haven't got any cases for you to help us with at the moment," said Ian the Inspector. "You've already solved all the cases we had on the go."

"Oh..." I said disappointed. Perhaps if I hadn't solved all three of their most mysterious cases all on the same day, I might still have had something to do.

"We do need your help though," said Ian.

"Oh," I said again, except this time it was an interested "Oh" not a disappointed "Oh."

"As you know it'll soon be time for our annual Police Ball," continued Ian.

"I know that," I replied. "You're going to ask me if I'll do my amazing impersonation of a pigeon, like I did last year aren't you?"

"Well... not exactly..." said Ian. "Your impersonation of a pigeon was very...er.... interesting... but we thought this year we'd like something a bit entertaining... I mean different. We thought we'd hire a clown act. But you see that's our problem."

"I can't understand what you mean, there are loads of clowns in this town," I said.

"Well you see, the town clowns have found that we're looking for the best clown in town and they've told us they're not going to tell us who it is." said Ian. "We've got to find out which clown it is using clues. We've asked all our usual contacts but all of them have told us that if they tell us who the best clown in town is, the clown will do something really silly to them, like paint their garden orange."

"Oh," I said again. This time it was an "I don't know what to say except, "Oh" Oh."

"We haven't been able to understand any of the clues we've got and it'll be

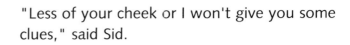

"Less of your cheek or I won't give you some clues," said Sid.

"Sorry," I said.

"All I can tell you is that the best clown's trousers are four times twenty centimetres long and that his top hat is four times taller than his bowler hat, which is ten centimetres tall." said Sid.

Next I went to see Totally Truthful Ted at the betting office. He was worried about the town clown's threat as well.

"If I tell you who the best town clown is, the town clowns have threatened to cover the front of my shop in chocolate so none of my customers will be able to find the way in," said Ted.

"Couldn't they make bets about where the door is?" I asked.

"Any more jokes like that and I won't give you any clues." said Ted.

"Sorry," I said (again).

"All I can tell you is that the best clown's silly shoes are five times longer than eight centimetres and his silly gun that shoots out a flag which says "BANG" is six times longer than four centimetres long."

After that I went to see Never Lies Larry, the landlord of the "Ball and Chain" pub. To my amazement he was worried about the town clown's threat as well.

really embarrassing if we can't track down a clown, let alone a criminal, so we're hoping you'll help us," said Ian.

"Even though I'm disappointed that you're not going to ask me to do my impersonation of a pigeon again, I'll help you," I said. "I'm sure my contacts won't let a silly threat from the town clowns worry them."

I was wrong (for once.) I first went to see Very Honest Sid who owned the second hand car garage.

"I can't tell you who the best clown in town is," said Sid. "Because the town clowns have threatened to cover all my cars in strawberry jelly if I do."

"Won't it make it easier to sell your cars if the customers can't see them properly?" I pointed out helpfully.

"If I tell you who the best clown in town is, the town clowns have threatened to put baked beans in my pipes instead of beer, so all my customers will end up with pints of baked beans instead of pints of beer. It'll look horrible." said Larry.

"It'll still taste the same though won't it?" I asked.

"Listen, if you're going to be rude about my beer, I won't give you any clues," said Larry.

"Sorry," I said (yet again).

"All I can tell you is that the best clown has got three times as many stars on his jacket than circles and twice as many suns than moons."

Finally I went to see Good Gail who ran the hair saloon. I knew she wouldn't be put off by a silly threat of silliness. I was wrong yet again.

"If I tell you who the best clown is, the town clowns have threatened to put salt and vinegar in all my shampoo bottles, so all my customers will smell like a bag of chips when I've finished doing their hair," groaned Gail.

"Doesn't that mean they'll smell delicious as well as look gorgeous," I asked thinking I was being helpful.

"Only a man could make a stupid joke like that," groaned Gail. "If you say anything else stupid I won't give you any clues."

"Sorry," I said even though I couldn't understand why Gail didn't find my joke funny.

"All I can tell you is that the best clown has got four times as many custard pies to squash in peoples faces as jugs full of custard to pour down their trousers. Also he's got six times as many banana skins to slip on as horns which make silly noises."

Well, with all those clues I thought I could work out who the best clown in town was. I worked out who I thought it was in the end, even though it took me a long long time. How about you see if you can work it out between you and see if we agree? I've given your teacher a copy of the details about the town clowns, which Ian the Inspector gave me. When you've done that I'll tell you what happened next.

To read when children have completed challenges

I agree with you the best clown in town was Blobbo! It was hard to work out though wasn't it! You needed all the clues! Well Ian the Inspector was very pleased with me and gave me a free ticket to the Police Ball. I really enjoyed it even though half way through his act Blobbo poured custard all over me. He told me that I wasn't supposed to tell the police who the best town in clown was either!

The End

Sailors setting standards

Programmes of Study
KS1. Ma 3. 1b select and use appropriate mathematical equipment when solving problems involving measures or measurement.

Ma 3. 4a. … compare and measure objects using uniform non-standard units (for example, a straw, wooden cubes), then with a standard unit of length (cm, m), weight (kg), capacity (L) (for example, "longer or shorter than a metre rule", "three-and-a-bit litre jugs)…

Lesson plan

"To explore the use of non-standard and standard measures."

"To investigate measuring things using non-standard and standard units."

"It is important to understand the difference between standard and non-standard units."

The stories and worksheets given here could be used together or separately, the first story leading to work exploring the use of non-standard and standard measurement of length and the second for weight (and in either case there's also a worksheet to support exploring the measurement of capacity.) The investigations could be organised on a carousel basis, which would no doubt make it easier with regard to acquisition of resources (there's rarely 15 balances available in most schools for 15 pairs working together!) The work could lead to a class discussion about the problems associated with using non-standard measurements and the advantages of using standard measurements.

Resources

For measurement investigations
Cereal boxes, books, bog roll tubes, pencils. Metre ruler. Centimetre ruler(s). Tape measures.

For weight investigations
Baked bean cans, bags of potatoes, lumps of plasticine. Assortment of standard sized and non-standard sized materials to weigh them with e.g. marbles, counters, cotton reels, coins, nuts and bolts. Balance scales. Gramme and Kilogramme weights.

For capacity investigations
Assortment of containers that the children can fill with water e.g. toy bucket, bowl, watering can. Mugs/cups etc. of varying sizes for the children to measure their capacity with. Measuring jug clearly marked in Litres.

Further ideas

Class activity
The children could all be asked to measure the distance across a particular area e.g. the playground/field/hall in paces. Each result could be recorded by the children or the teacher. Back in the classroom the children could place their result as a block on what will build up to be a class graph. (Number of paces against number of children).

Individual activity
The children could write their own versions of stories explaining how standard units of measurement and weight came to be used, or as it is not explained in either of the stories how standard units of capacity came to be adopted! Alternatively these ideas could be explored as a drama activity as a class/group.

Name: _____

Measure the height of your friend using a set of the same objects.
Here are some of the things you could use.

boxes   books   tubes   pencils

If your objects will stack you could measure your friend standing up.
If they don't your friend could lie on the floor to be measured.

What objects did you use? _____

How many did you need? _____

Measure your friend again with some more of the same objects.

How many this time? _____

Did you use the same number? _____

Were your objects easy to measure with? _____

Why? _____

Now measure your friend using a metre stick or a tape measure.

What was the measurement? _____

Now measure your friend again.

What was the measurement this time? _____

Why do we measure using metres and centimetres?_____

_____

_____

Worksheet 2: Wonderful weighing and brilliant balancing

Name: _____

Choose an object to balance.

You could choose:

Teddy   Book   Tub of pencils

Choose some smaller things to balance it with. You could choose:

Marbles   Coins   Nuts and bolts
Counters   Cotton reels

How many of the small things did you need?_____

Weigh the object again, using some more of those small things.

How many of the small things did you need this time?_____

Was it the same number as last time? _____

Were the small things you chose good to use? _____

Why? _____

Could you have chosen anything better? _____

What?_____

Now weigh your objects using kilogramme and gramme weights.

How much did your object weigh?_____

Weigh the object again.

Did it weigh the same?_____

Why do we measure in grammes and kilogrammes?_____

Name: _____

With a friend choose a container.

You could choose:

Bowl

Bucket

Watering can

Both choose a different cup.

Measure how much cups of water it takes to fill the container.
Fill it once with your friends mug and then once with yours.

How many of your friends cups did it take to fill your container? _____

How many of your cups did it take to fill the container? _____

Was it the same? _____

Why? _____

Now use a litre measuring jug.

How many litres did you need? _____

Try it again.

How many litres did you need this time? _____

Why do we measure in litres? _____

Sailors setting standards

Or "If I have to walk the plank, how long be the plank?

Now listen up shipmates… I mean classmates… I be going to tell 'ee a tale that was told to me by that famous sailor One Nose Pete. One day as we were sitting on empty barrels, watching ships enter and leave the harbour, he did turn to me and say, "Now you listen here Mad About Maths Mick, I've seen many things and heard many lies in my two hundred years as a sailor. I've come across… pirates!!! I've been shipwrecked more times than I've been in a ship. But I've never heard or seen anything as strange as the tale I be going to tell you now…

The story be of two crews of sailors who did bravely leave the comfort and safety of their homelands and set sail to search for lands none of their kind had ever clapped eyes on before.

One group of sailors were called the Squares. They bravely sailed the wild and windy Circular Sea to see what new lands they could discover for their King, King Quadrilateral. They did face… storms at sea… they had to fight huge creatures with tentacles a kilometre long that did come up from the depths of the sea to devour them that they had to fight off

with their cutlasses and blunderbusses… they ran out of food… then… nearly the worst fate that can befall a crew of sailors… they began to run out of fresh drinking water… they became so thirsty they thought they were going to go m… m… maaaaaaaaaad…

Just as the brave Squares set out to sea, so did some other brave sailors called the Triangles. They bravely sailed the stormy Octagonal Ocean to see what new lands they could discover for their Queen, Queen Equilateral. And they did face… hurricanes which fair threatened to rip their ships to driftwood… they had to fight huge beasts that did come up from the depths of the sea to devour them like sharks with teeth ten metres long that they had to fight off with their cutlasses and blunderbusses… they ran out of food… then… nearly the worst fate that can befall a crew of sailors… they began to run out of fresh drinking water… they became so thirsty they thought they were going to go m… m… maaaaaaaaaad…

Just as Captain Square, the Captain of the Squares thought he was going to go cr –

cockadoodle doo – razy, he was able to say to his shipmates… "Ahoy, shipmates! There be an island ahead on the horizon. Let us go and land on it and name it Square, after us." (For you see shipmate, all explorers are big heads and name as much as they can after themselves.)

Just as he was saying this, on the other side of the island, Captain Triangle, the Captain of the Triangles thought he was about to go ma – moo – ad. But then he was able to say to his shipmates… "Ahoy, shipmates! There be an island ahead on the horizon. Let us go and land on it and name it Triangle, after us!" (As I just told you all explorers be big heads.)

So soon after Captain Square jumped onto a beach on one side of the island, the very first Square ever to set foot upon the island. As he did so he declared, "In the name of King Quadrilateral, I name this island Square!" Then he turned to his shipmates and said, "Come on shipmates! Let us go and see if we can discover the natives that do live on the island and tell them it's got a new name!"

Just as he was saying this Captain Triangle was wading onto a beach on the other side of the island, the very first Triangle to ever set foot upon the island. As he did so he declared, "In the name of Queen Equilateral, I name this island Triangle!" Then he turned to his shipmates and said, "Come on shipmates! Let us go and see if we can discover the natives that do live on the island and tell them it's got a new name!"

So the Squares crossed the island looking for the natives that did live upon it. Meanwhile the Triangles were crossing the island from the opposite direction, looking for the natives that did live upon it. As it happens the island had no natives living upon it – or they were too smart to show themselves when these bigheaded explorers were bumbling about on it anyway. Finally though the two groups of sailors discovered each other.

"Shiver me timbers, shipmates," said Captain Square. "Look at those small strange natives that do live on the island!"

"Freeze me woodwork, shipmates" said Captain Triangle. "Look at those tall strange natives that do live on the island!"

Well shipmate, although the two groups of sailors were confused for a little while, especially as the Squares tried to tell the Triangles that the island was now called Square and the Triangles tried to tell the Squares that the island was now called Triangle, they soon learned each others languages and the confusion was resolved. In fact because they no doubt respected each others courage and resolve in being able to lead the harsh sailor's life, the two groups of sailors got on like a house boat on fire.

But after a fortnight of telling each other tales of the deeds they'd done at sea and about their beloved homelands and rulers, it was time to think of returning home. As they began discussing this, Captain Square did say to Captain Triangle, "You know shipmate,

when I get home my King will ask me all about you. As I've got to know you, I've realised how like us you Triangles are... For, you love laughing – just like we do – though it helps you to cry sometimes when you're upset (just like it helps us sometimes as well). You love working hard... even though you pretend you don't (just like we do!) So the only real difference between us is that we Squares be really tall and you Triangles be really short. The only trouble is I can't think of a way of explaining to my King how much taller we are than you and how much shorter you are than us. We haven't had that problem before."

"That be right, shipmate," agreed Captain Triangle. "I've got the same problem, except the other way around. I need to think of a way of explaining to my Queen how much shorter we are than you and how much taller you are than us. We've never had that problem before either."

"Hmmm," mused Captain Square. "Well cart off my cutlass." He wasn't quite sure if that was the same problem, except the other way around, or just the same problem. "Anyway shipmate, what are we going to do about it?"

"Well pickle me parrot, I've got an idea!" declared Captain Triangle. "Look at these here coconuts that have dropped out of the trees growing around the edge of the beach. Why don't we stack them on top of each other and see how many coconuts tall we are?"

"Singe me sail, that be a great idea!" boomed Captain Square excitedly. "Let's do it!"

So they did. Well shipmate, they did discover the first time they measured each other that Captain Square was ten coconuts tall and Captain Triangle was six coconuts tall.

"We'd better check these measurements shipmate," said Captain Square. "For it be a long way to come back if we aren't sure and want to check it again later."

"That be a good idea shipmate," agreed Captain Triangle but when they measured each other a few more times to check their measurements with different coconuts, they found to their astonishment that often Captain Square was more than ten coconuts tall and sometimes he was less than ten coconuts tall. It was much the same with Captain Triangle. Usually he was actually less than six coconuts tall and every now and then he was more than six coconuts tall.

"Well bung up me blunderbuss! Why do we never get the same result when we measure ourselves with different coconuts?" shouted Captain Square in frustration. "These coconuts be driving me nuts!"

"It must be something to do with these here coconuts," said Captain Triangle.

The two sailors looked carefully at the coconuts. For ages neither of them could see why the coconuts kept giving them different results when they used them to measure with. Finally the doubloon dropped.

"Why paint me porthole! All the coconuts be different sizes!" declared Captain Square.

"Well cry in me crow's nest, you be right!" agreed Captain Triangle. "We need to measure ourselves with something which is always the same length."

"I know," said Captain Square, picking up a length of driftwood. "Why don't we use this here piece of driftwood. If we just use this one piece of driftwood, it'll always be the same length!"

"Well shave a shark, that be a brilliant idea. If we use the same piece of driftwood each time, our measures won't keep drifting off like they did with the coconuts! It will be a standard measure but what shall we call this measuring stick from now on as it'll become a special measure for sure?" asked Captain Triangle.

"Well, as we sailors met here on this island, why don't we call it a Meet-here Stick?" suggested Captain Square.

"Why lunch with a landlubber, that be a great idea," agreed Captain Triangle. Then he had a brilliant idea too, he got out his seafaring knife and cut a hundred equal length notches along the Meet-here. As "Centi" was a posh word for a hundred in both their languages, (like it is in ours) they called these little measurements Cent-Meet-heres.

Then they measured each other with the Meet-here Stick. To their amazement and delight they did discover that Captain Square measured Two Meet-heres and Thirty Centi-Meet-heres every time they measured him. Also Captain Triangle measured One Meet-here and Seventy Meet-heres every time they measured him!

"Put raspberries in me rum, we've found a way of always getting the same measurement!" said Captain Square.

"We certainly have! That there Meet-here Stick be a standard measure that we can always rely on," agreed Captain Triangle. "We'll cut all measuring sticks to the same length and mark them in the same way when we want to make more of them. So the standard will be the same everywhere! "Speaking of rum, let's go and have some (but only a sensible amount of course)!"

So they did shipmate and that was how the standard measurements we use today were invented. Of course their names have changed a bit over the years as the tales been passed on from sailor to sailor. Some of them like to embellish the tales with ideas of their own you see, most of which are barefaced lies. Not me of course, for I never lie. Now then shipmate, did I ever tell you of the time I fought the terrifying octopus with twenty tentacles?

The End

Using stories to teach **Maths** *Ages 4-7*

Or "If I be worth me weight in gold doubloons, what weight might that be?

The day after One Nose Pete had told me the tale about the Squares and the Triangles, we were sitting outside a pub near the harbour, called "The Pretend Pirate", drinking matured apple juice.

I was just about to ask Pete if the rumours were true that the pub was named after him, when he turned to me. "I suppose shipmate, you want me to tell you the tale of how the Squares and the Triangles said their goodbyes when they were ready to leave the island they'd both discovered at the same time."

"I… er… um…" I said, not knowing until then that there was a tale about that.

"It goes like this," continued One Nose Pete. He never listened to anything I said. "A couple of days before the Squares and the Triangles were ready to set sail, Captain Square decided that he wanted to give Captain Triangle a gift to take home with him to present to Queen Equilateral. Explorers always think giving gifts makes them look civilised and never think it has anything to do with them showing off. Well cut my toenails if I be telling a lie but at

exactly the same moment Captain Triangle decided that he wanted to give Captain Square a gift to take home with him to present to King Quadrilateral. He thought that would show King Quadrilateral how civilised the Triangles were and didn't for one moment think of showing off.

Not once thinking about showing off, Captain Square decided to give Captain Triangle the biggest gift he could think of. Well clean out my ears if I be telling a lie; it was a huge silver cube. It was so huge it took two strong sailors to heave it along to Captain Triangle's camp. Meanwhile, not once thinking about showing off, Captain Triangle decided to give Captain Square the most expensive gift he could think of. Well give me my first bath for twenty years if I be telling a lie; it was a really expensive gold pyramid. It was so expensive two strong sailors were on duty to guard it as it was carried along to Captain Square's camp.

Now you can pick all the dead flies out of my beard if I be telling a lie, but as Captain Square was arriving with his gift at Captain Triangle's camp with his gift and shouting, "SURPRISE!… OH… " Captain Triangle was arriving with his gift at Captain Square's camp with his gift and shouting, "SURPRISE!…

OH…" They'd gone to each other's camps by different routes!

Thinking he was being very clever, Captain Square went back to his camp, following the route Captain Triangle must have used. Meanwhile thinking he was being very clever, Captain Triangle was going back to his camp following the route Captain Square must have used. So when they both got back to their own camps there was no one else there any more!

"Banana-flavoured barnacles!" Captain Triangle declared as his exhausted crew collapsed. "I know, we'll be even cleverer. We'll wait here in our camp until Captain Square and his crew come back here." Unfortunately at that very same moment Captain Square was shouting, "Orange Octopuses!" as his exhausted crew collapsed. "I know we'll be even cleverer. We'll wait here in our camp until Captain Triangle and his crew come back here."

Well make candles out of the wax in my ears if I be telling a lie, but the two captains waited for each other in their camps for a whole day, without anyone going anywhere.

In the end Captain Square screamed, "Starry-eyed Starfish! This is getting us no where. I'll send a messenger." So he did. As it happens, at the very same moment Captain Triangle was screaming, "Hiccupping Haddock! This is getting us no where! I'll send a messenger!" So he did.

So in the end, the two captains finally met each other again.

SURPRISE!... OH…" shouted Captain Square as he presented his gift and then saw the magnificent gift Captain Triangle was giving him at the same time.

"SURPRISE!... OH…" shouted Captain Triangle as he presented his gift and then saw the magnificent gift Captain Square was giving him at the same time.

Neither of the captains said anything – because of course they'd never thought about it before – but they both secretly thought that the other captain had managed to show off more than they had… (not that they'd been intending to show off of course…)

"Performing porpoises, this gold pyramid be a lovely gift. Thank you," said Captain Square recovering himself and remembering to be polite.

"Singing swordfish, this huge silver cube be a lovely gift. Thank you," said Captain Triangle also recovering himself and remembering to be polite.

The two captains and their crew admired the wonderful gifts.

"Paint me poop-deck purple, you've been very generous. For gold be worth far more than silver," said Captain Square to Captain Triangle.

"Well you can pour gravy over me galleon, I think you've been far more generous than us, for that silver cube be far bigger than our gold pyramid," said Captain Triangle to Captain Square.

"No, no…" began Captain Square. And so the two captains spent the next half an hour telling the other captain how much better the gift each of them had received was than the gift they'd given. So in the end they ended up being far more polite than they had been envious for a moment, which made them both feel better about themselves. We're all allowed a moment of weakness at times. Even when they'd finished being polite, they still stood admiring the two wonderful gifts.

"You know, having compared all the ways these two gifts be different from each other, I can't help wondering how much heavier the silver cube is than the gold pyramid," said Captain Square.

"Well peel a plum on me port-side," replied Captain Triangle. "That was exactly what I was wondering."

"Eat a stew in the stern, how amazing," said Captain Square. "So how are we going to find out how heavy these here gifts are?"

"I've got an idea," said Captain Triangle. "Why don't we use the pebbles on the beach? We could make a kind of see-saw with a plank of wood and then see how many pebbles it takes to lift up the silver cube and

then how many pebbles it takes to pick up the gold pyramid!"

"Take hold of me hold, that do sound like a great idea!" declared Captain Square. Now you can scrape out the mud out between me toes if I tell a lie but although Captain Triangle didn't realise it he had just invented the world's first weighing scales!

So they tried out Captain Triangle's idea and his see-saw scales worked. They weighed the silver cube and they found they needed seventy pebbles to lift it up the first time they weighed it. Then they weighed the gold pyramid and they found they needed thirty pebbles to lift it up the first time they weighed it. But remembering what had happened when they tried measuring themselves with coconuts; they weighed the presents a few more times to check, using different pebbles. To their astonishment they found that sometimes the silver cube weighed more than seventy pebbles and sometimes it weighed less than seventy pebbles. It was much the same with the gold

pyramid. Sometimes it weighed less than thirty pebbles and sometimes it weighed more than thirty pebbles.

"Well sail off with me sail! Why do we never get the same result when we weigh these gifts with the pebbles?" shouted Captain Square in frustration.

"It must be something with these here pebbles," said Captain Triangle.

The two sailors looked carefully at the pebbles. They had seemed to be about the same size before they'd looked properly but then Captain Triangle had the brilliant idea of seeing whether thirty pebbles on one side of the see-saw scales balanced thirty pebbles on the other side of the scales. To their surprise they didn't.

"Well clap while you clap me in irons," declared Captain Square. "All the pebbles must be a different weight from each other!"

"Well cut me with me cutlass, you be right!" agreed Captain Triangle. "We need to weigh these here gifts with things which are always the same weight."

"I know," said Captain Square. "Why don't we try these gold coins we use for money and these heavy gold bars we use for making the coins with? If the gold coins and the gold bars weren't all exactly the same weight then I'd have a mutiny on my hands every time I paid my crew!"

"Well puff up me pistol, that do sound like a good idea," said Captain Triangle.

So they checked the coins and thirty coins on one side of the see-saw scales did balance thirty on the other. Also one gold bar balanced another gold bar. As the Square's coins were called grammes they decided that should be the name of the small coin weights they were using. As one gold bar turned out to weigh the same as a thousand grammes

• • • • • • • • • • • • • • • • • • *Using stories to teach* **Maths** *Ages 4-7*

and "Kilo" was a posh word for a thousand in both their languages, they decided to call the gold bar weights Kilogrammes.

Then they measured the gifts. To their delight they did discover that the silver cube weighed twelve kilogrammes and four hundred grammes every time they weighed it. Also the gold cube weighed five kilogrammes and a hundred grammes every time they weighed it!

"Well double me doubloons, we've found a way of weighing things so we always get the same result!" said Captain Square.

"We certainly have!" agreed Captain Triangle. "These weights are acting as a standard. Well shipmate, looks like it is time for us to say goodbye and go and tell our Rulers what we've discovered."

So they did shipmate. When they got back to their homelands, King Quadrilateral was delighted with his gold pyramid and Queen Equilateral was delighted with her silver cube. But of course both the monarchs were much more excited to hear about the way the sailors had worked out a way of measuring each other so that you always got the same measurement and that they'd worked out a way of weighing things so that you always got the same result. Still, that's understandable isn't it shipmate, for there be hardly anything more exciting than Numeracy be there? Apart from another of my true stories. Now did I ever tell you of the time I had a boxing match against a shark. It went like this…

The End